Rags to Riches

By: Joshua Scott Zeitz

A Story of God's Unfailing Love

Copyright © 2018 By: Joshua Scott Zeitz
Poetry/Rap: Joshua Scott Zeitz
Photos: Joshua Scott Zeitz

Cover Illustration:
"Transformed" By: Tolik Trishkin

Designer: Nora Marie Apple
Editor: Mark Apple

All rights reserved. Do Not Copy.

Scripture quotations marked KJV are taken from the
HOLY BIBLE, KING JAMES VERSION (KJV), public domain.

Scripture quotations marked WEB are taken from the
THE WORLD ENGLISH BIBLE (WEB):
WORLD ENGLISH BIBLE, public domain.

Some names and identifying details have been changed
to protect the privacy of individuals.

Printed by CreateSpace, An Amazon.com Company.
Available from CreateSpace.com, Amazon.com,
and other retail outlets.

ISBN: 1983821292
ISBN-13: 9781983821295

A Love Letter to my Best Friend – My God
Tuesday, February 6, 2018

I wanted to take some time before anything else in this book to simply brag upon my God! The young man you are going to read about in the first part of this book and even into the second half is gone! I have been made new. This is not some one-time profession or a ploy to sell books. This is raw. It's real. Jesus Christ is my Lord, my Savior, my Friend, my God.

Without Him, I am nothing. Without Him I am lost. Every single day He shows me His love and I get the opportunity to shower my love on Him as well. Every single day I hear His voice and I know that He loves me. I have a relationship with the same God who created the universe. I have a relationship with the same God who was hung on a cross to die over 2,000 years ago. He was raised from the dead for me!!!

I have heard His gentle voice calling to me in some of the darkest times of my life and yet I have also heard His praise when I make right choices, when I choose to serve Him and to put Him first. He has blessed me beyond measure, more than I could have ever imagined. Yet, this is only the beginning. I get the opportunity to walk alongside Him every day. He never leaves me or forsakes me. He is a constant friend and help in time of need.

He comforts me when I am hurting. He cheers me up when I am down. He loves on me even when I don't deserve it. He is my best friend. He tells me secrets hidden from the world and whispers in my ear in the night and in the morning. He is so intimate and full of compassion. I would be lost without Him. I was lost without Him.

"Father, Daddy, I love you! You are so awesome and wonderful, and I magnify you today, right now! You are my best friend. Thank you so much for who you are. I just want to love on you right now and tell you how much you mean to me. Thank you for saving me – for transforming me – for adopting me into your family.

Thank you, Father, for the opportunity to write this book and to share the greatness of your Love with others! Thank you! Thank you for allowing me to write the raps and poems within as well and for ministering to me through them time and again.

Thank you for all those who will read this book and be blessed, healed, saved, and forgiven as a result of it. Thank you, Daddy, for providing all my needs according to your riches in glory in Christ Jesus! Thank you for family, for friends, for health, for joy, for Jesus, for the Holy Spirit!

Father, I love you! As the deer pants for the water brooks, so does my soul thirst for you! (Psalm 42:1) You are my hope! My salvation! My God! Thank you! I praise your holy name. I adore you and exalt you above every other name and every other thing in my life.

Your love never changes and I'm so grateful to you. I love Father, Daddy!

In Jesus' name I pray.
Your son, Joshua"

This book is dedicated to my beautiful wife, Mitzi, who has been by my side through the best and worst of times.

CONTENTS

PART I

	Forward	VIII
1	The Beginning	1
	Rap – *Love's Fantasy*	6
2	The Child Factory	8
3	The Best and Worst of Times	16
4	A Light on the Horizon	27
5	The Dream Continues On	33
	Rap – *ABC's of Shame*	40
6	Darkness Falls	41
	Rap – *Smaller*	54
7	The Great Awakening	58
	Rap – *Chasing Shadows*	62
8	A New Beginning	64
	Rap – *ABC's of God's Grace*	68
	A Letter from the Author	70

PART II

	Intro to Part II	80
9	Happily Ever After	83
	Rap – *Into the Light*	92
10	Mitzi	94
11	On the Move	100
12	Back to Reality	108
	Rap – *Put Him First*	116
13	A Fresh Start	118
14	Healing in His Wings	127
	Rap – *My Friend*	138
	Write It Out!	143
15	Joyfully Ever After	146
16	The IAh's Have It	159
	Prologue	169
	Rap – *Bye, Bye, Bye, to The Old Me*	176
	Write It Out!	182

ACKNOWLEDGEMENTS:

I want to thank Jesus first and foremost for
transforming my life and saving me.

My wife and children,
you are my life and my blessing from the Lord.
Thank you for believing in me.

Jody Thompson, my probation officer, for not just
doing her job, but actually caring.

Pastor Jim and Joy Church for not only teaching
me what to do, but also how to do it!

My Aunt Beth Fox for writing the
Forward for this book.

My Uncle Mark and Aunt Nora Apple for their help
in editing, designing, and publishing my testimony.

And, I also want to thank my adoptive Mom and Dad
for giving my brothers and me a home
and rescuing us from the "system."

FORWARD

I can still remember the day that Raymond joined our family through adoption. I was his new adoptive Aunt. What an amazing event to watch these three brothers, who had been separated in the "system," now be rejoined as a family-unit under a new roof in a home where they would be loved. Our family gathered many Sunday afternoons for the biggest dinners you could imagine made by these three youngsters and their new Dad. We celebrated many birthdays out at the grandparent's farm.

However, one memory I have of Raymond up at the lake, where we shared many fun family times together, was disheartening for it showed me the severity of the pain that this young boy was suffering. Several of us were in the speed boat when Raymond had an undeniable display of anger, rage, brokenness, and hurt all in one outburst. I knew at that moment this young elementary boy was traumatized from abuse and if it was not properly dealt with, he would be one out-of-control teenager. Raymond's new parents did the best they knew how, but only God was going to be able to truly touch his hurt and redeem his past.

Many years later when Raymond was in high school,

our family gathered again for one of our favorite times of the year, Christmas. Raymond, however, had gotten involved in the "wrong crowd" and with drugs. Consequently, he had hardened his heart toward our family. He willfully denied any gifts from us and absolutely would not darken the door step for any of our Christmas gatherings. Raymond wanted nothing to do with any of us, or so we thought.

The darkness that loomed around Raymond seemed to thicken. Increasingly I felt an evil presence whenever I tried to reach out to him. It was evident that he hated life, but most of all, he had grown to passionately hate his adoptive Mom. She had become the scapegoat for much of his pain. Initially what had seemed like such a great family to Raymond had broken into shambles. By this time, his adoptive Mom had moved to California trying to start a new life.

Another year passed and it was the Christmas season again. His Mom excitably planned her trip home to Indiana for all the Christmas festivities. Since Raymond had nothing to do with any of the family gatherings the year before, we assumed he would stay away yet another year. His rebellious life had heightened and his drug intake was no less than a perfect match for disaster. Raymond despised his Mom, so why would he come around if she was going to be there?

On a crisp December morning, I was awakened by two vivid and horrific dreams from which I could not shake the heaviness. Immediately all I knew to do was to rebuke them. I quoted scriptures and claimed God's protection. The seriousness of these dreams stayed with me. Both dreams were about Raymond brutally killing his Mom, my sister! I was mortified! Would Raymond do something like that? Surely not, but I was not naïve to the fact that with the brain altering drugs he was addicted to, mixed with all the rage inside of him, anything could happen. I continued to rebuke it!

My husband, two small children, and I were moving out of state on New Year's Eve that month, so there were many people we wanted to personally say goodbye to before we made the move. One Friday evening, my husband and I met with a young pastor and his wife for a goodbye dinner. During our conversation, the topic of spiritual warfare became the central focus. Without even taking a breath, I began sharing the burden of these dreams that I was carrying. I was only into the beginning of the first dream, when this young pastor's wife quickly stopped me, only to insist that her husband tell me what she had dreamed the week prior.

This couple had never met Raymond, didn't even know anything about this situation, but in her dream, she saw blood flowing down the driveway of the farm (where we would be having our Christmas gathering). This couple had only been out to the farm once, so it was not as though they were close family friends. The farm was the same location in one of my dreams where Raymond had tried to kill my sister, his Mom. We stopped and said, "I think just as soon we're finished eating, we need to go out to the car and PRAY!" And that is exactly what we did!

I called my sister and told her everything, so that if she wanted to opt out of coming home for Christmas, we would all support this wise decision. However, she prayed about it and decided to still come. Obviously, we continued to pray! My husband and brother had a gun in the back closet just in case Raymond made any unannounced visits.

Well here it was, Christmas day! My sister and her new family were at the farm and we were all enjoying the visit when the phone rang and Raymond's older brother, William, called and said he was stopping by. Nothing was mentioned about Raymond, but I knew he wouldn't come, since he had no interest. He seemed to hate Christmas, and us too.

A few minutes later, I headed to the back door to greet William, and to my SURPRISE Raymond was with him. My heart started pounding. I couldn't believe it. Was I living out my worst nightmare? I wistfully tried to cover all that was swarming in my head, so I gave William a hug and then Raymond one as well, but Raymond kept his hands in his low-rider jeans' pocket.

All I could gather was that he was holding a gun. I followed them into the kitchen giving my husband all the signals behind their backs as we had rehearsed. Raymond was as cold as ice to his mother, but PRAISE THE LORD he did not even attempt what I had dreamed. Could those dreams have been a wake-up call that sent all of us to our knees? I believe so! I have never, before, nor since had such vivid and unsettling dreams.

God is a REDEEMING GOD! In this book, you will see how God took a broken and enraged young man and met him where he was and gave him LIFE...new life, a redeemed life!

I am in awe of Jesus' perfect love for each of us. Raymond's life is a beautiful example of what Christ's love can really do...forgive us, adopt us, and free us! As you read this book, open your heart and allow GOD to speak to you.

Praise God,
Beth Fox (Aunt Beth)

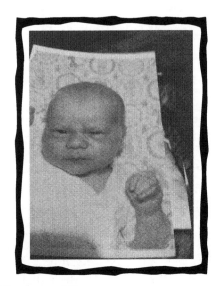

Part I:
Rags to Riches

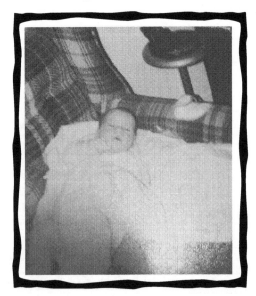

1 "THE BEGINNING"

The sirens could be heard in the distance. He sat listening, wondering, and waiting. Where will they head this time? Blaring sirens were not exactly an unusual thing in Indianapolis, Indiana. They were a daily occurrence. Sometimes they could be heard numerous times a day. There always seemed to be some sort of commotion going on. He sat, looking out the window, unsure of life. Unsure of anything really. When would his mom be back? How long did they have to stay here this time?

He was used to waiting for his mom to show up. It seemed she always had some errand to run or somewhere else to be other than with him or the other children. He had two brothers and one sister. He had always been the loner of the family; the thinker if you will. Not that they didn't think, mind you, but he seemed to always be somewhere else.

Take today for instance. He sat alone thinking of the sirens he heard of which were drawing closer by the minute. Maybe today he would see some action. It couldn't, and wouldn't hurt anything. After all he sure wasn't seeing much action around there. The house he was in was bustling with activity for sure; his siblings were playing with the other children. They were all yelling and screaming. It seemed to him that they were playing tag or something. Yet, he didn't care too much. He just sat and listened and waited. His mind was a million miles away.

This house was a usual drop off place for his mother. It was only a few blocks from home and the adults of this place were friendly enough. He wasn't sure if they were family or not. To him, it all seemed so strange. It seemed they were here more often than not. His home wasn't much of a home at all. It was more like a meeting place to gather supplies or to sleep in on occasion. He was never too sure where his mom would disappear to all the time. He just knew it happened often.

The sirens were growing louder now. He could see patrol cars turning the corner. There were two of them. He was going to see some action today. He wondered who they could be coming for. Perhaps there was a fugitive on the run in the area. Or perhaps they were going to do a drug bust? He could only guess as he inched himself closer and closer to the window for a better view. It was then that he noticed the adults of the home standing at the door as if they knew something he did not. They looked saddened for some reason. Suddenly it hit him. Maybe something happened to his mom and they were waiting nervously, expecting some sort of bad news? Everything seemed to grow very quiet in the house. A hush fell on everyone inside. It was as if everyone realized at that same moment that the sirens were not of passing patrol cars searching the area. They were not the usual noise of the neighborhood. They were a reality now not just background music of the city. The two patrol cars turned off their sirens as they pulled in the drive. Their lights were still whirling around but no more sound was emanating from them. It was as if the whole world went silent.

Then, without warning, the silence was broken. The sound of the front door creaking open could be heard. The adults of the home both walked outside together. They stood there in the drive, silhouetted by the morning sun, talking to the policemen. There were no tears, no looks of astonishment, or of surprise. It was becoming increasingly clear to Raymond that the conversation taking place outside was not one of a sudden catastrophic event. Even though he was only four years old he could tell.

He could tell that the adults of the home had been the ones who beckoned the officers. But why all the sirens and the sense of urgency? This was no emergency call. This was a planned visit. The police officers looked blankly at the adults of the home who looked saddened but relieved as well. What was going on? What were they saying? All the little minds of the home pondered the same thing. By this time, all the children had gathered around the large front room window. They were all peering out at the spectacle outside.

Then, as if in one unanimous decision, all four adults outside turned and headed toward the house. Raymond sat paralyzed thinking back on the day before. That was when he had last seen his mom. He remembered how she had dropped them off as if she was only going to be gone for a couple of hours or so. She had mentioned something about going to the grocery store. It always seemed odd to Raymond that she never took them with her. Occasionally, she would take the eldest two, but never did she take Jonathan or Raymond. Jonathan was Raymond's younger brother. They were two years apart. Jonathan seemed oblivious to all the commotion. "Raymond, Jonathan." "Raymond, Jonathan!" "Come here!"

Suddenly Raymond snapped back to reality. The woman of the home was calling his and his brother's names. They wanted the brothers to come to them and the policemen standing in the foyer of the home. He sat unmoving, not sure what to think. Jonathan went immediately of course, without a fear in the world. It was strange for Raymond to have such a fear at just four years old, but nevertheless, he was frightened. He was not sure at all what to think of this whole thing. It became very clear to him that those policemen dressed in their whole attire of guns, badges, clubs, handcuffs, and dark blue pants tucked into their big black boots were there to take him and his younger brother away.

He wasn't sure why, but they wanted the two boys to go with them. He could hear the policemen mumble something along the lines of "Oh, it's going to be alright. It's ok. We're not going to hurt you." Of course, the policemen talked to these two young children as if they agreed with them; as if at their age, they should just automatically know what they were doing and where they were going and what was going on. But they didn't. Raymond cried. As he cried Jonathan cried also.

Suddenly, as if in a tornado, the two boys were swooped up and hauled over to the giant cruisers sitting in the driveway. They were both placed in the back seat of one of the vehicles. Another officer, sitting in the passenger seat, was there to greet them as they were buckled in the seats and the doors were shut. The two officers that had carried the two boys to the vehicle walked back over to the adults of the home with pen and notebooks. They were scribbling something down looking very important and official as if this kind of thing happened all the time - maybe it did. But it's never the same when you hear the sirens somewhere else.

The officer in the passenger seat handed each of the

boys a pack of ball cards from the glove box. It was his feeble attempt to quiet the young children who were still weeping in the back seat. The driver's side door opened and one of the officers who hauled the two boys away took his seat behind the wheel. He turned around and told the two children to quiet down or else he was going to take away their cards. How did he know they both had cards? He just got into the car.

It was obvious now. That glove box was chock full of ball cards and this was not the first time these two officers had made this sort of stop before. The car backed out of the drive and headed down the street. Raymond could barely see the outlines of the adults of the home standing in the drive as the cruiser passed out of their view.

He did see some action that day. However, this was a little too close to be fun anymore. He sat back and closed his eyes. Perhaps when he awoke it would all be over and he would be seated back inside that old house on the corner staring out the window waiting, wondering when his mom was coming back…

"Love's Fantasy"

Eyes closed as I float through life,
I'd look up but the sun's too bright,
So, I grit my teeth and I hold on tight
to these memories that are flying by.
Time's fading fast,
thru this hourglass.

Wake me up I can see right through it.
Don't wake me up cause I just might lose it.
Love's fantasy is all I see.
What's real is real right in front of me
the hurt, the shame, the pain and the suffering.
Love's fantasy is all I see, tonight.

I look away, but it just keeps pressing.
I want to stay, but I just can't face it.
I drift away and I can't get past it.
Love's fantasy is haunting me, tonight.

I slip away, but I come back to it.
I hideaway, but you see right through me.
I push and pull, but your love's enduring.
Eternity is chasing me, tonight.

Open my eyes.
Open my eyes.
I'm scared, I fear
to open my eyes!

Love's fantasy is all I see.
Your mercy beckons, calls to me.
Love's fantasy is all I see.
Your precious blood was spilled for me.
I'm crying out, down on my knees.
Love's fantasy
it calls to me, tonight.

Eyes open, it's a brand-new day.
I look up and I see your face.
The futures gleaming, so I hold on tight
to the one who gave me life.
Love's reality
is all I see, tonight!

   By: Joshua Scott Zeitz

2 "THE CHILD FACTORY"

The car came to a screeching halt outside what appeared to be a giant factory looking place. It was old and scary looking, especially to a four-year-old child. The policemen didn't seem to pay any attention. As soon as the cruiser came to a stop the two officers hopped out and opened each rear passenger door. The seat belts were unfastened and the two boys were hauled inside the old scary looking building.

A lady, with glasses, sat with neck craned to the side staring at papers, busily typing away as the officers dropped off the boys in the chairs waiting for them in a room to the side of a long corridor. Just like that the officers were gone. Perhaps they had to go and get some more children. Raymond didn't know. He didn't care. All he knew was that he did not want to be there.

It all seemed so formal. It was like this whole ordeal was rigged from the beginning. Everything was working out according to someone's master plan. It was a factory thought Raymond. It was a factory where they made children. It had to be. He thought to himself, there must be thousands of children in this place.

The lady stopped typing and peered at the two boys over the rims of her glasses. She began asking questions right away. This was all too planned. Everything moved so quickly. Maybe they thought that these children didn't have any feelings? Maybe everyone thought if they just finished everything quickly they would not have to feel either. Perhaps at one time these people did feel, but over time, with all the things they had seen, they had become numb. Whatever the case may have been Raymond was scared and he did not know how to communicate these feelings.

He had already begun his numbing out process. He had to. Between his mom always being gone and the sexual abuse he had already gone through, he had to learn at a very young age to block out certain things. Those things included trusting people. He trusted no one. Everyone was his enemy. Everyone who ever attempted to care about Raymond had either abused him, someone else he knew while he watched, or they had abandoned him.

"Young man!" The lady was now close to yelling towards Raymond. "What is your name young man?" The lady kept repeating herself. "Ray-mo-nd" came the pathetic voice of the child. He never spoke too much. He didn't like to. It was one of his defenses. If he didn't talk to anyone they couldn't find anything out about him and they couldn't get to know him more. And if they didn't know him or talk to him or come around him they could not hurt him. Life was far too complicated for young Raymond.

He worked hard at staying off the radar. However,

weren't normal children his age supposed to be on the radar? They always were in some of the movies he watched on television. They seemed to be the center of attention with the all the ooohs and ahhhs and hugs and kisses they were always getting. It wasn't normal for a two and four-year-old to be discarded, ignored, and pushed to the side - or was it? He didn't know. However, it was what Raymond had become accustomed to. He never experienced the love and attention the children on T.V. received.

He could remember one birthday party he attended. He wasn't sure if it was his or someone else's. He got one of those fake fishing poles - the ones with the big plastic fish tied to the end of the line instead of a hook. He could remember sitting at the top of the stairs and casting the line into the imaginary water at the bottom of the steps. He would always catch the same thing, but he didn't care. At least he got something of his own.

Of course, it was that same memory that was invaded with the thought of all the adults gathered around the table yelling at each other and playing poker at the party. He remembered getting passed something in a little cup from one of the adults to drink. It tasted funny to him and it burned his throat. Not until later did he realize they were giving him beer. They probably thought it to be funny in their drunken stupor. They would pause at least long enough to blow out the candle on the birthday cake. He remembered there being a single clown birthday candle on the cake. It was one of those real big ones with party dots all over it.

That was about the extent of the happy memories that he had. Granted he was only four, but surely normal kids had better memories than his? He wasn't sure. By the looks of the place they were at now, it seemed that all children were treated the same. Perhaps all children were ignored until they were old enough to join in the poker games and drinking parties?

There was a grandpa that Raymond remembered eating breakfast with every morning. He would sit and play cards with him and serve him breakfast in bed. One morning Raymond went to wake up his grandpa, but his grandpa did not move. He would not get up. He just laid there motionless and lifeless.

Later he learned that his grandpa had died in his sleep. Raymond was not allowed to go to the funeral. He had to stay home with his older sister. Maybe his mom thought he was too young for such events. All he knew was that the only person he had to play and laugh with was gone.

His other grandpa used to let the children watch dirty movies whenever he babysat them while their mom was out doing "errands." He knew they were dirty movies because every time a bad part would come up his grandpa would make them cover their heads with these plastic orange baskets left over from trick-or-treating. Raymond remembered the people on the screen were always getting naked or being killed. One time he even saw a child get hit by a semi-truck and then he came back to life. He later realized that his grandpa was letting him watch porn as well as horror movies.

Once the lady was done with her questions, the answers of which Raymond didn't remember giving, she led the two boys into a large room with what seemed like rows and rows of beds. She showed them where they would be sleeping and then she gave the two boys a brief tour of the building.

Raymond was not sure what to do because this lady rambled on like they were expected to remember all her instructions. He didn't remember too much about that scary looking building that he thought was a factory for children. He just knew that the adults who roamed the factory hallways and talked to him made him feel uncomfortable. They were always asking questions. He hated questions because they always involved answers. And answers involved talking. And he hated talking to people he did not know.

The day finally came for Raymond and his brother to leave that place. Two months had passed since their arrival. He was surprised that he could stay with his brother. He hadn't seen his older brother or sister since he and Jonathan were taken by the policemen at the house on the corner.

There was one adult that always seemed to talk to the two boys at the big scary place. She said she was evaluating them; whatever that meant. Apparently, she was attempting to match them with the best suited foster parents. That same lady was the one who took them away from the big stone building. She drove them to a big house in some neighborhood. The lady said that the adults in that home would be their new parents. At least, they would be for a little while. She called them foster parents.

The adults in that home seemed friendly enough. The man of the home was never seen too much. There was a younger girl that lived in the house. She was the adults' daughter. She was probably ten years old or so. Raymond could remember the adults always telling him to go and play with her. It seemed wherever she went he had to go. He did not like that very much. Besides, the girl seemed sort of snobby to him.

It was probably another one of the system's attempts at fixing young Raymond. They always had something they were trying to fix in him, on him, or around him. The "system" was what Raymond would learn to call this whole process of moving from foster family to foster family and in and out of that old scary building.

When he got a little older he learned it was called the Guardian's Home. It was an orphanage for abandoned and neglected children.

Raymond used to pee the bed in that first house he and his younger brother were sent to. The parents would get so frustrated with him. He was, after all, almost five years old now. He couldn't understand why he did it. He tried not to, but it was no use. Apparently, it's not uncommon for children like him to wet the bed. It has something to do with the traumatizing events that take place in the child's life such as sexual or physical abuse.

Raymond and Jonathan were not at that house very long. They were moved around a little more after that before being sent to the last foster home they would stay at. The walls in Raymond's heart were growing higher and higher each day. He was constantly learning new ways to cope with all the emotions that whirled around inside of him. Sometimes it seemed as if they would just burst out all at once. But he would never and could never let that happen. He had to protect himself from any more harm. He knew it was impossible, but he tried anyway. He would learn how to shut people completely out. He would learn how not to care. He would learn how to deal with whatever else life had to throw at him no matter the cost.

He was learning alright, but he wasn't prepared for what was to come at the next stop in his life. It would be the last foster home he and his brother would visit. It would be a place of confusion, more hurt, more sexual abuse, more pain, and more building up walls. It would also prove to be the place where a major change would occur in Raymond's life. That, however, would have to wait. That would not come until the end of his stay there. Until then, he and his brother learned what life could really be like in a foster family.

Below and right are excerpts taken from the "Book of Me", which were written or drawn around 1990, before Raymond was adopted. They were part of the file that the "lady of the orphanage" (a.k.a. his caseworker) compiled from Raymond's assessments.

Left: This drawing is of Freddy Krueger, one of the many horror movies he would watch as a child with his grandfather.

Right: This drawing is Raymond's rendition of the lake in northern, Indiana.

Why I Don't Live with My Birth Family

Becose they stade out to long at are ants houes. Than the cops came but we ditn't hafe to go the first time. They told us that if are parrit at home by 11:09. Than ther come back to take us to the gardeishom. They were not home by the time that the cops told us so they came back and took us to the gardeishome.

Young Raymond while in Foster Care, date unknown.

3 "THE BEST AND WORST OF TIMES"

They pulled in the drive of their new home seated in the back of the four-door sedan belonging to the lady at the orphanage. She assured them that these were nice people and this would certainly work out better than the previous homes. She said these people even go to church every Sunday and they have other small foster children living with them. They would fit in just fine. Unsure of whether the lady was being completely honest or if she was reading off her usual line when she had to drop off another package of children, Raymond decided to try and think for the better. After all, he was getting older now. He was beginning to realize that he had to be strong for Jonathan. He and his brother would be calling this house their home, so they may as well attempt to make it work.

The lady of the guardian's home had talked with Jonathan and Raymond several times. She even took them out for ice cream on occasion. Her purpose was to try and help the two boys. She would ask them all sorts of questions about their short past and about their memories of their mom or dad. Jonathan was much too young to remember anything and Raymond would only answer in one or two word answers like "fine" or "good" or "bad", or things like that. No matter how many ways she asked the same questions, how many ice cream cones she bought, or how many notebooks the boys filled out with silly little facts in them, Raymond remained shut off from the world.

After all, this was his only form of defense. This lady was trying to tear down the walls he had so delicately and diligently attempted to keep standing, and to keep building for that matter. It seemed that all her work was futile. No amount of psychotherapy could cure young Raymond's aching heart. Even though his physical heart was young and thriving his soul was growing older day by day. It seemed that Raymond was getting sick. He didn't think about that side of things. He just knew that if he let out any of his feelings, he would only suffer more hurt.

As they pulled in the horseshoe shaped drive, Raymond could see some of the other children playing at the side of the house. They were kicking balls, swimming in a little pool set out in the yard, and some were even riding bicycles. He wondered how many other children lived there. Instantly he began to take mental notes from the things that he saw. He would need these mental notes to determine his best means of coping in this new environment.

The house seemed rather large to him and there was a decent sized garage to the right of the far end of the driveway. He even spotted a shed in the backyard. "Were these people rich?" thought Raymond. Of course, everything does tend to seem a little grander to someone who is only five, about to be six in October. Perhaps he would have his own room? He thought about these things as he was filed into the owner's front room.

He was introduced to the adults of the home. They greeted him with warm smiles. They promised the two boys that they were going to enjoy living there.

Raymond smiled and nodded. He already had his routine picked out whenever introduced to new people, especially adults. He would half-heartedly smile and nod his head. He thought it best not to talk, and yet not to come across as too rude. He didn't want them getting any silly notions about splitting up him and his brother.

After all, Jonathan seemed to always be smiling. Raymond was sure it was because he was so young. But even as Jonathan got older he always seemed to have a certain air about him. He could always light up a room with his ear to ear cheesy grin. The adults always thought it was the cutest thing; that is until they saw how much of a handful Jonathan could be on more than one occasion! Raymond remembered back to the time that Jonathan had poured milk and cereal in some of the cribs back at the Guardians' home!

He remembered the time while staying at another home that he walked in the room while a teenage boy was ripping up Jonathan by his hair in his crib. Raymond was defenseless. He just watched as Jonathan screamed out in pain. Apparently, the teenage boy didn't like his crying so he thought it was best to try and rip his hair out to shut him up. They were used to these types of harsh and irrational behaviors from adults.

Raymond even remembered the times that his mom would lock him and his younger brother in their bedroom in the morning. They used to get up early and sneak food from the cabinets. They were hungry and didn't want to wait for their mother to get out of bed. (There was no telling when she would wake up, especially if she stayed out quite late the night before.)

She would lock the boys in their room to prevent this thing from happening. She could not afford to have them raiding the cabinets. The boys would use the restroom on their bedroom floor. It did not matter whether it was number one or number two.

Raymond remembered sitting there on his fecal stained carpet rocking back and forth against the bedroom door chanting, "Let me out, let me out." Raymond loved his mom and was not sure why she did such things. He never resented her until later in his life. At the time, he was naïve to the rejection that was being deeply enrooted within his heart.

Suddenly Raymond snapped back to reality. He was always drifting off in thought. He didn't know how he got there, but he was in what was to be his new bedroom. The adults of the new home were giving him and his brother a tour of the place. Not surprisingly, he would not be getting his own bedroom. He was going to have to share the room with three other children.

They showed the two boys the rest of the house and then they sent them off to greet and play with the other children. They proceeded to talk to the lady from the orphanage. Raymond remained distant from the other children. He would remain that way for quite a while. It always took him a long time to read someone, analyze them, and then finally approach them.

He was not one for quick introductions. This home did seem to be quite different from the other places he had stayed at. Maybe he would like it after all. Little did he know the secrets that lied behind the façade that was placed up to impress this lady from the guardians' home.

The lady said her goodbyes to Jonathan and Raymond. She assured them one last time that this place would be good for them. And then she told the two of them to behave. After giving each of them half a hug, she was on her way. Raymond watched as her vehicle pulled out of the drive, down the road, and out of sight. He wondered how long it would be before she'd come back to do the whole process again.

The adults of the home sat the two boys in the living

room. They began to give the boys the run of the place, complete with a verbally stated set of rules. The two boys tried to listen best as they could. It was a little difficult, especially with the other children peering in on them from the other room.

That was when Raymond first noticed her. She sat in the shadows of the adjoining room. Behind her hung posters on the wall. "That must be her own room," Raymond thought. Finally, as if the adults were reading his thoughts, they asked the older girl to come out and introduce herself. She walked out of the room and told the boys that her name was Amanda. The adults of the home introduced themselves as Betty and Jack. They said that Amanda was their birth child.

They introduced them to other children as well. There was a little girl there whose name was also Amanda, a boy named Terrell, another little girl named Alex, and another boy named Josh. They said that Josh was also their birth child. Raymond tallied the children in his mind. There were two birth children, three foster children, and he and Jonathan; seven in all. The home was packed to its limits.

As the weeks went by, Raymond got used to life around that house. He was beginning to feel more comfortable around the other children as well. He did notice, however, that the two birth children of the home were treated better than the rest. They always got prime seats in the car, the best food, and the best toys. In fact, Raymond did not remember having any toys of his own. Anything that he may have received was tossed into the community chest for all to share. He did not mind that so much. He just thought it odd that the other two children, Josh and Big Amanda, did not have to contribute to the chest. (Big Amanda was what they called the eldest girl since there were two Amanda's in the home.)

There was even the one time that all the children were gathered around the table eating lunch. They were eating chicken nuggets. There was one last nugget left. Raymond was still quite hungry and thought to himself that he'd better go ahead and snatch the last one before anyone else did. It was probably selfish of him but he didn't care. He wanted that nugget!

However, he was not the only one eyeing that last morsel. Josh also had his mind set on that last bit of food, and he had a trick up his sleeve. He went in the other room and asked Jack if he could have the last nugget. He was sure that that would silence all debate between him and Raymond. After all, Josh always got his way.

Dad and son walked into the kitchen and much to Josh's dismay, the nugget was gone. Raymond had seized the opportunity when he left the room. His mouth was full of the remains. Instantly, Raymond was catapulted into the air with his back to the ceiling. Jack did not like the fact that anyone would put one over on his son. He was screaming at young Raymond. "Why did you eat that last nugget without asking?" Frozen in fear, Raymond said nothing. Without warning he was tossed to the floor. He was sent scooting across the tile where he came to a stop under the table.

He sat there crying, unsure of what to do. He was defenseless. The other children watched as he sat quivering on the floor. This was not the first-time Big Jack had blown up on the children. It would not be the last. It was best to just keep quiet and wait for the moment to pass and that is what everyone did.

Betty had her moments of rage as well. All the children called her the Pepsi queen. It seemed that every time you looked at her, she was drinking a Diet Pepsi. She would sit in her chair and watch television sipping on a huge glass.

One time Raymond walked in on her as she was giving Jonathan a whipping. Her face was beet red and sweat was pouring down it. She was a rather large woman and the sight was ghastly. She sat with Jonathan across her knees whelping his bottom. It seemed to Raymond like forever before she was done. She looked as if she was going to pass out. Jonathan was screaming at the top of his lungs.

Apparently, Jonathan had been caught playing behind the garage. Raymond knew he was also playing out there the day before with his brother, but Jonathan never told on him. He was thankful for that. Of course, Betty would never have spanked Raymond. She always spanked Jonathan instead.

It seemed that he was the whipping boy for the two of them. I guess she figured that with spanking Jonathan she could get away with it. After all, Jonathan would never tell a soul. He was shut up easily with candy or toys. That always bothered Raymond.

Jonathan always seemed so happy even after all the beatings he received. Perhaps he just got used to them or maybe he too had his own form of coping. Raymond wasn't sure, but he never liked watching it occur. It would be one thing if he was just spanked for doing wrong only, but it seemed that everyone always had to take it way too far with him. They always had to let out all their anger on the young child.

Life at Jack and Betty's was different, to say the least. You never knew which personality was going to greet you on any given day. One day they would be the most loving people that Raymond had ever encountered. They would take the children to the grandparent's house down the road or to the candy shop, or to church. The next day they would be tyrants with a list of rules that never seemed to end. And if you screwed up, you would be punished fully.

Then sometimes it seemed that they were never around. They would both just disappear. Raymond wasn't sure where they went. Maybe they just wanted to get away from it all. Their lives had to be hard at times taking care of so many children. It was during these times that they would leave the children in the care of their oldest child; Big Amanda. It was during these times that Raymond would be introduced to yet another realm of what foster homes can be like.

Big Amanda was not unlike her parents. She too had her mood swings and different days. Sometimes she would put music on the television and all the children would dance and have fun. Raymond remembered learning moves to Paula Abduls' Dance Step videos. Big Amanda could be the most fun person to be with and yet sometimes she could be the meanest girl that you ever knew. She would use the restroom in front of the children as they sat eating in the kitchen. She made no attempt to hide anything in the process.

She took a fondness to Raymond. She would send everyone in the other room to play while keeping Raymond in the front room with her. There she would tell him that they were going to play house. She would be the mom and he was going to be the dad. She would have him lay on the couch with her while she took off his clothes and did things to him that he thought felt awfully strange and shameful. He did not want to make her mad by pulling away. After all, she would tell Betty and Jack how bad he had been.

Raymond remembered the movies that his grandpa used to make him watch in the house in Indy. Maybe this was normal thought Raymond. He just didn't know why it felt so dirty. He knew that Jack and Betty slept naked sometimes with their door open. Maybe Big Amanda was just acting out what she had no business seeing in her parent's room. Whatever the case was, Raymond wished he could run away. But he couldn't. He felt trapped.

Raymond knew that Jonathan would somehow take the punishment later from the adults if he said anything. He never told on Big Amanda. He just built up another wall and tried to push away the pain.

It wasn't long before he began acting out what he and Big Amanda did with little Amanda. She was about the same age as Raymond. He would gather all the children in the room in the back of the home. He would tell them all that they were going to play house. He would be the dad and little Amanda would be the mom. All the other children would be their children.

Little Amanda and Raymond would crawl under the bunk bed in the room and proceed to act out what Big Amanda had done to him. Raymond knew that what he was doing was wrong. But he somehow pushed the feelings away. He even began to like going under the bed. A whole new world had been opened to young Raymond. It would prove to be a world that would haunt him for a very long time.

The weeks that followed at that home passed by rather quickly. That place was sure different alright. It had proved to be a place of ups and downs. It was the most fun place at times and the darkest place at times. It was the safest place and yet the scariest place. Raymond had learned a lot at that house. He learned how to ride a bike, play baseball, and skate down on a slip and slide on his belly in the heat of the summer. He even made friends with some of the children there. He watched broken-hearted as he saw some of them leave whom he had gotten close to. He knew how they felt. He and Jonathan had been there before. He greeted new children as they came in. He learned more about people.

He learned how different they could be. He learned how nice and yet how evil some could be.

Some of the things he learned at that house were things that no child had any business knowing, let alone any adult either. He had been through a lot. Through it all, Raymond had experienced new feelings of happiness, shame, pain, hurt, rejection, fear, disappointment, sorrow, and he built new walls and went further into himself. To Raymond, it seemed that life was one big disappointment. No matter how many people that he got close to, they always seemed to let him down in one way or another.

If there was one word to describe how he felt in this new home that he and his brother had been at for over a year now it would be: confusion. There were too many mixed emotions, mixed up people, and mixed up situations to try and sort through.

It was here that Raymond learned that people, in general, could not be trusted. Sure, they were fun at times, but in the big scope of things; people were evil and awful creatures.

He would lay in bed at night and rock back and forth. He would rock for hours at a time. Whenever someone would walk by or make a noise he would stop rocking and act as if he was asleep. To him, his rocking was shameful. He thought people would think it strange how he liked to rock in bed. For that matter, he was ashamed about a lot of things. His self-esteem and self-image were nonexistent.

He would talk to his pillow at night. He used to act like it was his girlfriend. He would kiss it and hold it. He would even get out of bed in the night and sneak food back to bed and act as if he was sharing a meal with it. To him this pillow was the only one he could talk to. It is not uncommon for children like him to take food in the night. It has something to do with their traumatizing past.

One time he took a cookie jar full of Oreos. He ate all of them. He woke up and vomited all over the place in a feeble attempt to reach the restroom. He went back to bed too scared to say anything about the incident. Boy, did he ever hear it the next day! They made him sit on a stool in the corner all morning. He wasn't sure why he was the way he was; talking to pillows and rocking in bed. To him it was his little secret. He had his own little world that he would close himself off in. There he could be anyone or anything. There he could hide from his pain and troubles. It was there that he would learn to stay for a long time.

4 "A LIGHT ON THE HORIZON"

Almost two years had gone by at Jack and Betty's when something strange happened. It was wonderful and strange at the same time. One day some people showed up at the house. There was a man and a woman and a young boy of about nine or ten years old. The boy said that he was Raymond and Jonathan's brother. Raymond looked in awe. It was his brother! He was so excited to see him. He wasn't sure why they were there but he was glad they were.

The boys ran all over, as if in a frenzy. Jonathan and Raymond gave the full tour of the yard. They kicked balls, hit balls, played tag, and even threw the Frisbee. It had been three years since they last saw each other. For the first time in a long-time Raymond felt a sense of hope. He did not know why, but he liked the feeling. He didn't want them to leave. He asked his older brother William what he had been up to. William said that he too had been in foster homes and then one day these same people came and began visiting with him. They said that they wanted to adopt him and so they did. William told him about all the troubles he had had at the homes he went to.

Raymond just stood there and listened in

astonishment. Perhaps these people would take him and his brother away from this life as well. Perhaps they would be rescued from all this torment and moving from home to home. The adults that had adopted William came out into the yard and introduced themselves to Jonathan and Raymond. Their names were David and Mary. They asked the boys if they could come and visit them. They wanted to get to know them more. Jonathan and Raymond agreed.

Raymond was a little more hesitant, of course. Even though these people had adopted William, he still wasn't too sure if they could be trusted. He would have to get a feel for them first. But on the inside Raymond was leaping for joy. He was so excited at the prospect of possibly getting out of the "system". They all said their goodbyes. As they were getting into the car they promised the two boys that they would be back soon to visit them. Raymond still wasn't sure whether to believe them or not. Maybe they didn't like him. Maybe they wanted different children instead. Whatever the case, Raymond held on to that faint hope that William had given him.

Once they left and were gone, Jack and Betty told all the children to go inside and wash up for supper. They didn't seem too pleased at the whole situation.

Raymond avoided eye contact with them as he entered the home. In the back of his mind he hoped that they were telling the truth. For once he hoped that someone would tell the truth. He already longed for them to return. He wanted so badly for him and Jonathan to be taken away. As he lay in bed that night he thought of what it would be like to live with a real family. He tried to imagine having actual parents. His imagination was immediately stifled. He realized that he had nothing on which to base any of his contorted thoughts. That evening's sleep was a restless one.

He awoke in the night and looked out his window. His eyes were wide now. He saw something coming towards him in the yard outside. It looked like a man with something in his hand. He was wearing overalls and had a mask on his face. He was moving closer and closer getting faster and faster. To Raymond's horror he realized that it was Jason from one of the scary movies he had seen with his grandpa in Indianapolis. He screamed out in agony. He awoke to someone smacking him on the bottom. They were trying to wake him up. He had been having a nightmare.

A week or two passed by and Raymond saw a car pull in the drive. It was the same car that had brought his older brother William. He was excited.

David and Mary got out of the car and went up to the house. Raymond watched out the window in the front room. The adults were all whispering. Jack was hesitantly nodding his head to some proposal that David was making. Then he and Jonathan were called into the kitchen where all the adults were talking. Jack asked Raymond if he would like to go with David and Mary for a trip in their car. Raymond and Jonathan both silently agreed, nodding their heads. It all seemed to happen so fast.

The boys began visiting with David and Mary on a regular basis. They would go to their house, their church functions, out to eat with them, to the zoo, to the park, and wherever else David and Mary took them to. It all seemed like a dream to Raymond. There were never any deep conversations or outpourings of hearts, but they did have fun together. Raymond and Jonathan hated going back to the foster home. They would always cry and beg David to let them go with him.

David would often stop at a gas station on his way to

drop them off. He would buy them all sorts of food. They would eat ice cream, hot dogs, candy, pop, chips, and whatever else they could stuff down their throats on the trip back to Jack and Betty's house. Raymond loved the games they would play in that old truck as well. David would tell the boys that the truck would blow up if anyone ever took the key out of the ignition while the truck was moving. Then he would act as if it was an accident as he ripped the keys out while they were blazing down the highway. Jonathan would always scream out in fear. Raymond laughed hysterically.

They also used to play freeze out and burn out. Here they would either get the truck super-hot or super cold and they would see who the last man was standing. Of course, if it was extremely cold in the truck the thing to do was to take off your shirt just to prove that you were hot and wished someone would turn on the cold air.

The three guys would have a blast on those trips back to the foster home. The trip back always seemed to go by so quickly to Raymond. He never wanted to leave, but would always cling to hope in the next visit as he went back to the foster home. Jack and Betty never seemed thrilled to have the boys back at the house. And they would never let the two bring anything back with them. Raymond dreamed of the day that he could live with David instead.

It seemed like time was flying by. David and Mary were going to take in Jonathan and Raymond to live with them. They wanted to see how the boys would cope being in a new environment. They would stay there for a week or so. The boys were visited again by the lady of the orphanage. She asked them all sorts of questions. She wanted to make sure that the home was fit for the boys to live in. She also wanted to make sure that Raymond and Jonathan were comfortable living in this new home.

Raymond offered little help to the lady. He did however agree to live there. That was really all she needed. It was all part of the process of adoption. Time passed and all parties involved came to the unanimous decision. The boys were to be adopted by David and Mary. They all sat in the courtroom in their best clothes. Raymond and Jonathan had on brand new clothes given to them for the occasion. The judge asked them both if they wanted to be adopted by David and Mary. They both agreed.

Finally! The boys had been freed from the system. No more moving from home to home. No more scary looking children's factories. No more Big Amanda. No more visits. No more sleeping in the same bed with two and three other children. They had been rescued!

David and Mary had bought a new home. They would be moving into a new house with new parents. They would be a part of an actual family. All signs pointed toward a new beginning and a fresh start for the boys. It was true. Raymond's wish had come true. He and his brothers would all be together. There was a definite burden lifted from young Raymond with this new beginning.

However, this burden was only one of many burdens that weighed down on the boys. Up to this point, it all seemed surreal. Lurking in the background of all this excitement were hundreds of horrid looking black creatures. It was almost like they were waiting for the right moment to strike.

In all the excitement, there was still the one thing that everyone had neglected to do. The boys had a lot of baggage. On the outside, they were only five and seven-year-old sweethearts. They were poor innocent children that had been rescued from a life that no child should ever have to go through. They even looked happy. No one seemed to notice the black creatures that consumed these boys. They were invisible to the naked eye. But they were very real. These ugly, morbid creatures were all the junk that came along with these two boys. They were the shame, the hurt, the pain, the abuse, and all the mess that the boys had buried deep within their hearts.

The walls that Raymond had worked so hard to build were still standing strong. To Raymond, he hoped that they would just somehow disappear. He did not want to disturb any of the creatures lurking in the dark. They were scary and they could cause a lot of hurt. So, he locked them up. Way back in the deepest parts of his being he locked them up. He somehow thought that that would be enough. Never again did he want these demons to get loose.

Little did he know that up until then these demons had given him a false sense of power. They had allowed Raymond just enough control to build up the walls that they could live in. They used him to build a home for them. Now they would show him who the real boss was. Slowly, one by one, they began to take hold of Raymond. He would become their puppet. Ever so slowly though. They still wanted to keep that false sense of power in the forefront of his mind.

5 "THE DREAM CONTINUES ON"

In the next few years that passed, the dream that Raymond had found himself in seemed to continue onward. He had all but forgotten that old life he used to have in the "system." At least he tried to. He was learning to like this new family he had. Some might say that he was even beginning to love these adults that had so generously taken in him and his brothers. At least he loved them in whatever sense he could at that time.

However, there was an emptiness in Raymond's heart. He did not know how to describe it exactly. If he could have tried, he would say that it was an uneasiness and an unhappiness if you will. On several occasions, he caught himself thinking of his earlier years as he lay in bed at night. It seemed like so long ago. Here he was at twelve years of age, five years after being adopted into this new family, and yet he could not cleanse himself from a past that seemed to grow on him each day.

It was an indescribable blackness eating away at him. He tried to push it away. It had always worked in the past, why wasn't it working now he thought? It was as if this blackness had a life of its own and it was growing stronger as the years passed. It was beginning to choke him. He could feel it and yet was defenseless to stop it.

He could try and call out for help, but what would people think? After all, he had a new life now. There was no need in bringing up the past, or was there? He did not want to disappoint David and Mary; not after all the kindness they had showed him. Plus, no one ever seemed to ask questions either. I guess if they think everything's ok, then it must be, thought Raymond. Perhaps this feeling will pass. That was it, it would pass. He just needed to wait a little longer was all. He lay there on his top bunk pondering all these things as he slowly drifted off to sleep. This became a usual occurrence before rest would come to Raymond.

David and Mary used to take Raymond and his brothers up to a lake in northern Indiana. It was there that Raymond had some of his most fond memories. From the age of seven to fifteen Raymond visited the lake a lot. They would go fishing, tubing, swimming, hiking, boating, and do all sorts of fun things.

It was during this time that he really began to bond with his new dad. He was not sure when exactly he began to call these new adults in his life mom and dad. It just sort of happened, although it did take a little while. They didn't mind too much. They were just happy when the boys did call them mom and dad. But Raymond never bonded too close with his new mom. There were a few times that he would talk to her or snuggle with her on the couch or even miss when she wasn't there to tuck him in at night.

He even remembered crying one time because he awoke and the sudden realization hit him that he had been asleep and missed her coming in the room and making her nightly rounds with the boys. However, as he grew older, he grew more and more distant from her. He learned to resent her. Not that it was her fault, mind you. He just didn't like women in general. It had to do with his past dealings with them.

His new dad, on the other hand, was much easier to get along with. He was always doing fun stuff with the boys. He was the one that always came up with new ideas to live life to the fullest. He never tried to get personal with Raymond. And for this, he was appreciative. Anyone that could hide as well as Raymond from any emotional longings of the heart was game in his book.

His mom always tried to pry too much. Plus, she was always trying to throw a bunch of religious mess in his face. Something about God's love she would say. Raymond didn't care about all that. He just wanted to hide and have fun. He had learned to love being secluded from reality. In the years that followed he would learn other ways in which to run from reality as well. But for now, he was content to be a child. He was content just to go fishing, boating, play sports, and do things that he only dreamed about back when he was in the "system." He felt so alive.

David even taught the boys to cook. Every Sunday after church David and the boys would rush home and fix an extravagant meal. They would have people over all the time. The boys thought David and Mary were the richest people ever. They were always buying things. They had cars, clothes, boats, and toys. They had everything.

They even got an air hockey table, a ping pong table, and a computer for Christmas one year. On the outside looking in their lives looked great. Here was a family that had come together through incredible odds.

Raymond even got involved in Bible quizzes at church. There was even one time where he and William were moved deeply by a sermon at a church function they went to. Mary was there. She, William, and Raymond all hugged and cried together. Everything was really looking up. Hope sprang forth in Mary's heart. She hoped that this would be the turning point in her relationship with Raymond.

Up until then she felt like she was always pushed to the back burner with the boys. She was always the one who would suggest them going to church. She was the disciplinarian of the family. She wanted them to know this love of God she always talked about. But to Raymond he did not feel loved at all by her. He took her questions and her concern as personal attacks. He used to walk the halls at home and push her out of the way.

He and the other boys would throw snowballs at her on Wednesday night when she tried to get them to go to their church a mile down the road. One time she even had to get the State Trooper, who lived in the neighborhood, to come and tighten the reins on the boys. Each year they were all getting harder and harder to control. No matter what she did Raymond's hate for her grew stronger. He resented her very presence around him. He stopped talking to her altogether. This went on for months at a time.

She was slowly being pushed out of the picture and out of the family. So, you can only imagine her relief as they all hugged and cried together on that church retreat. She thought that things were finally going to get better. She had been praying hard after all.

Unsure of what sparked it, it happened. The fairy tale proved to be just that. A few weeks later Raymond was back with a fury. This time he would not let her get to him. This time he would hate her even more. It seemed the demons that ruled young Raymond's heart went into full attack mode as soon as any headway was made that showed the possibility that they would lose control of their puppet. This time they would make sure that no one interfered again.

The bait was placed in front of Raymond and he took it hook, line, and sinker. What was the bait? "That was not real." "It was all a fake." "You were not really changed at that youth retreat." "It was all a scam to try and get you to be weak." "It was a ploy to control you." As the thoughts persisted in Raymond's mind of what the children at school would think of his sudden conversion to this Jesus character, fear gripped his heart. He began to believe the lie: He was not really changed and his new mom was no mom at all.

From that point on, he would only call her Mary. In fact, if he had it his way, he would never talk to her again. He found his scapegoat and the demons regained their control. They came back with a vengeance. They would have to punish Raymond for his disloyalty. They would have to show him who was really in charge. Raymond's fourteenth birthday approached. And with it came an onslaught of evil that he had never experienced up until that time. For the next five years, all hell broke loose in young Raymond's life and this newfound family of his. The black creatures that lingered in the background came to the forefront.

It was time. They attacked with full force. All the strings were in place and they played their puppet masterfully...

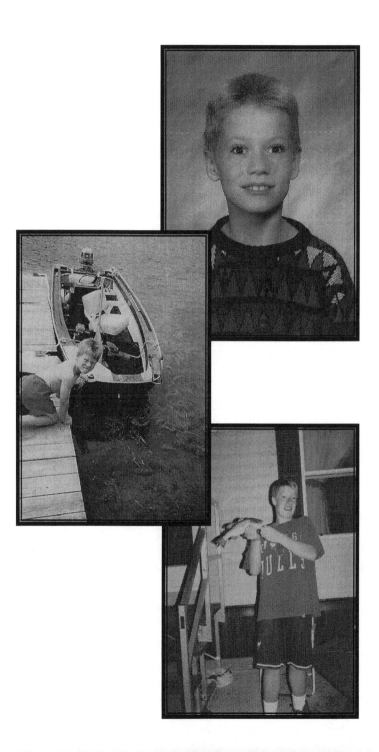

"The ABC's of Shame"

Addicted to self, I was vain
Balled up and chained
Couldn't change, I was strained
Drained of life
Eroding in my ways
Forgiveness was made
Grace was laid
Hope was feigned
I denied the change
Jesus, I denied your name
Killing me with shame
Lies were trained
My heart was stained
Nodding my head to the pain
Over and over again
Pleasure seeking my gain
Quickly they regained control of my life
Readily in the forefront of my brain
Stuck like adhesive I remained
Trapped in the storm
Under the rain
Veering out of control
Wishing I could change,
X out my life, I was lame
Yearning for love
Zapped by lust – so ashamed...

By: Joshua Scott Zeitz

6 "DARKNESS FALLS"

Raymond sat in the back of the little Ford Fiesta. It was parked behind a tiny tan colored house that belonged to a buddy of his at school. The boy's mom was at work and the three of them took full advantage of yet another opportunity. In the front driver's seat sat Luke and in the passenger seat sat Danny. Raymond grabbed the joint and inhaled deeply.

He wasn't sure how he came to be here. Well, he knew that he had ridden his bike there. He just wasn't sure why. He had been coming here for about a month or so and getting high after school. His new found "friends" were much too eager to welcome him into their little clique. He liked the feeling he got when he was high. The whole world seemed to make sense during those times. He was out of touch with all reality. To him, this was what he always wanted. He began coming here often. He was sixteen years old now.

He was so lonely inside and these new acquaintances were all he had. He enjoyed their company. That was the lie he told himself. In all actuality, he hated them and he hated himself. In the past two years, his adoptive parents had split up. They never were very intimate with one another. Raymond could count on one hand the number of times he saw them even hug each other. He wasn't sure of all the details of their divorce. In Raymond's eyes, his mom, that he hated, had run off with a guy she met at work. And his dad was never around too much either.

A couple of years earlier he and his brothers found out that David was hiding vodka in different places around the house. He tried to hide his addiction, but they all knew. William was kicked out of the house and Jonathan was also beginning to get involved in drugs. That was thanks to Raymond who got Jonathan high for his first time at a buddy's house across town.

At the time, it was funny. But inside of Raymond there was an intense battle going on. He hated himself for getting his brother hooked on pot. He got William high for his first time as well. That happened at a party that Raymond threw at the house when his dad and younger brother were out of town. During the next couple of years, things just kept getting worse. Time seemed to stop. Everything from that point on just ran together in Raymond's mind. He was always getting high and skipping school.

As Raymond sat there stoned in the backseat of that car, he began to think. He thought again of his childhood. He thought of his adoption. He thought of the times that he would swim with David under the boat up north. He thought of the times he played soccer and basketball in the optimist leagues. He thought about the times he would come home after church and cook with his dad and brothers.

How did things go so bad? Was it his fault? He felt like it was. At least he felt partially responsible. Maybe if he would have listened to his mom about all that church stuff. Maybe if he would just have said no that first time when he was asked to get high. Perhaps if he never found that vodka bottle or faced his dad about it. What could he have done differently? He pondered these things. Yet, he was powerless. He was on a downward spiral. And there was no end in sight.

Raymond was always bright in school. Up until high school he even liked attending. He remembered how excited he was when he got the honor roll in fourth grade. He made a cool pioneer project that same year. It was a log cabin made of pretzel sticks and it had a lake made of toothpaste.

He loved sports as well. All the boys excelled in sports. Soccer was Raymond's specialty. And he loved basketball as well. He wanted so bad to be on the high school team. He tried out, but he didn't make it. The next year he told the devil that he could have his soul if he would just let him get on the team. He never did make it. Little did he know that the devil already owned him.

High school proved to be a huge battle for Raymond. The school work was relatively easy for him. It was just that he was having troubles at home. His dad was becoming more distant. He always had a special bond with David. But David had his own troubles with his own dad. His dad, Raymond's grandpa, was a huge gambler and alcoholic. He ended up dying because of his lifestyle. Ever since then, David got more distant.

This man that meant so much to Raymond when he was younger was steadily becoming his enemy as well. He used to take long bike trips and walks with him. There were times that he and David would go out together, just the two of them, and eat. They got to be close, but as the drugs that Raymond was taking, took effect, his relationship with his dad, began dwindling away. Not to mention, David was beginning to drink more and more. Raymond had huge self-esteem issues. He hated everything about himself and he hated everyone else.

The evil that Raymond succumbed to grew worse in him. He began acting out sexually as well. The things that Raymond had gotten introduced to as a toddler reared their ugly heads once more. Raymond was addicted to pornography. He would even go so far as to steal his dad's credit cards and buy porn online. He used to practice phone sex on numerous occasions.

Every opportunity he got he was on the internet looking at porn or instant messaging various women on the internet pretending he was a different person. He would walk the neighborhood where he lived with thoughts of hurting women on his mind. When he wasn't practicing these things, he was hanging out with the people he knew getting high. He was turning into some morbid, hideous creature. He hated the person he was becoming, but the more he tried to stop, the more the evil all around him tightened its hold.

He had a job at a local pizza shop when he was only fourteen. He worked there for three years. However, as his drug use worsened, he was forced to quit that job. Raymond eventually was kicked out of his home. This was when he was seventeen. His mom, Mary, was already gone by then. She lived in California. William, his older brother, had been kicked out a couple years prior. David and Jonathan were the only two left in the house.

One evening, while Raymond was on one of his highs, he decided to spend the night at his dads. He needed a place to stay. He had exhausted all his other "friends." He hated everyone. Anyone that had ever tried to help him he ended up cussing out. He even made one of his buddies walk home one time because he made Raymond mad. He would throw his friends' CD's out the window while driving down the road if he didn't like them. He had no respect for anyone.

Well, this night he had nowhere to sleep. So, he

decided to sleep at his dads. His plan was to be gone by early morning so as not to awake anyone. His plan didn't work out. He ended up sleeping in. The car in which he was driving at the time was gone. It really wasn't his. David had let him drive it while he was living in the house. But when Raymond was kicked out he stole the car.

So, when David woke up that morning he decided to take the car and put it somewhere else. David was at work when Raymond woke up. Raymond called him on the phone and immediately began verbally assaulting him. He told him to come home right away or else. Jonathan was home at the time. Raymond proceeded to go about the home and break pictures, dishes, and furniture. Some of the pent-up rage within him came boiling out.

It was then that David walked into the house and Raymond turned on him in violent anger. He screamed and cussed at him. He threatened to kill him. He challenged his dad to fight him. Raymond was furious. He was angry at everyone and everything. David and Jonathan called the cops while Raymond persisted in threatening them. As they pulled out of the driveway, Raymond threw the phone at them and cracked the front window of the car.

At that point, he began to run down the street. He knew the cops were coming for him, and sure enough they did. They arrested Raymond for threatening and intimidation. Raymond was not sure why he did what he did. He just knew that he hated his dad now and he was beginning to hate his brother Jonathan as well. The same brother that he had tried so hard to protect when he was younger had now become his enemy.

Raymond turned eighteen in juvenile. He was immediately shipped to adult jail under the judge's orders and his dad's request. I guess they thought that it would help Raymond. It proved to be another factor in making him worse. Raymond used it to build his reputation at school. All his so-called friends thought he was a big timer. He had done jail time! To him, he was a nobody. He was so empty inside and he didn't waste any time at all trying to plug that hole. He immediately delved right back into drugs and pornography. This time he began throwing big parties when his dad was away. He began experimenting with different drugs as well.

One night, on his way to pick up someone for a party he was attending he saw flashing lights in his rear window. The cops pulled him over. They could tell he had been drinking. He was arrested and charged for drinking and driving while under the influence of alcohol. It was not uncommon for Raymond to drink and drive. This time however, he got caught.

He was getting more and more out of control. Upon his release from jail, his dad wanted nothing to do with him. So, he decided to go live with William. William was living in Indianapolis at the time. He had moved in with his older sister. Raymond wanted nothing to do with her. He was glad to hear that she moved prior to Raymond moving in. Raymond hated it there in Indy in that old upstairs apartment. But it was all he had.

The brothers were only in Indianapolis for a month before they moved to Greenfield. William had found them both a job. They would be unloading semis at construction sites. They managed to keep the job for one day before they were both arrested with the charge of Burglary.

Raymond and William got the bright idea to travel to their Aunt and Uncle's house and steal their computer. Then they left the computer in clear view for everyone to see. Of course, you don't exactly think straight when you're strung out on drugs now do you?

Raymond thought it quite foolish to be arrested on

such a bunk charge. But anyhow, this time it cost him six months in jail and a lengthy probation period of three and a half years since it was a Class C felony.

While in jail, Raymond caught a case of jailhouse religion. He tried to tell God that he would never do anything bad again if he would just get him out of jail. During his incarceration, Raymond got sober and gained somewhat of a clearer mind. However, his heart was unchanged. He gave lip service to fulfill his needs.

After being released from jail, he was happy to find out that he had a six-month-old pack of cigarettes in his pants pocket. He fired one up as he sat waiting on his grandma to come and pick him up. He attempted to convince her that he was a changed man and that he wanted to go down the narrow path now. She let him live there on her farm for a couple of weeks after he was released from jail.

Raymond's grandma prayed for him continually. She would always try and help him out as best as she knew how. He had so many good memories of her as a child. She was so excited when her daughter Mary decided to adopt the boys. Her farm was a place that the boys visited frequently when they were younger. As Raymond grew older, she was looked at as an enemy because Mary used to go over there every time the boys would send her out of the house crying. Raymond saw her as an accomplice to his mom. But, he could not be choosy now. After all, she was letting him stay there.

Raymond did not last long over at her house. He ran her phone bill so high with his sexual addictions that she had to have her phone shut off. To make matters worse, he ended up shooting her dog while she was away on a trip. He had overheard her talking about how old the dog was getting and how it kept killing the chickens, so he thought it best to get rid of the mutt with a .22 gun he found in one of the closets. It took five shots to finally kill the dog.

Raymond cried so hard after what he did that day. Of course, he never let anyone know that. When she found out what he did she was heartbroken, but he laughed about it. It was all part of the false façade that he attempted to portray to people. To those who knew Raymond at that time, he was death walking. He looked like it. He never smiled and rarely talked to anyone. He made it his goal to breathe hate towards everyone he encountered.

There was also the time that he had stuck a cat in the oven in Indianapolis. He sat and watched as the heat increased and the cat jumped in agony at the torture it endured. They say that most serial killers and rapists get their start with torturing animals. Raymond relished the thought of it. He welcomed evil like it was his best friend. Never mind the fact that it was this same evil that was tearing away at his soul.

When he was released from jail that third time, a buddy of his pulled up in his car. He told Raymond, "Hey I heard you found Jesus in jail?" Raymond looked sarcastically at the guy in the car and with eyes full of hate retorted, "Yeah, well I must have lost him." He laughed his deep angry laugh and got into his buddy's car to go get high.

Raymond used to make fun of this Jesus when he was high. He would curse God and anyone who had anything to do with him. It seemed that every time he did, something died inside of him. It was funny, no matter how much evil he got involved in; his heart always ached somehow whenever he cursed God. Perhaps it was the knowledge he had of him. Raymond didn't care, he would just get high some more to drown out the feeling of it all.

His drug use got so bad that he had to start stealing

to support his habit. He tried selling dope, but it never goes well when the seller consumes his entire product. He began breaking into cars around the neighborhood looking for change. He would go to his dad's house and steal money from him. He would go out to the farm and steal money from the milk barn where his aunt and uncle kept their money box.

The house in which he was living in at the time was the same small tan house that he began using drugs in at the age of fourteen. He was now eighteen and was living there with two of his buddies. The house was a wreck. There were animal feces strewn about. They had no hot water and he only had about two outfits to wear.

Where was the Raymond of his earlier years at his home in Fortville? He remembered all the money his dad had. He remembered how good he used to have it there. Now he was reduced to stealing to smoke cigarettes and eat food. These people he lived with were not friends at all. Every opportunity they got, they would get high without him so they wouldn't have to share.

Raymond's shame of who he had become kept him from asking for help. He absolutely hated himself. He would walk the streets until the wee hours of the morning alone. He thought about his life and who he was. He felt like a puppet in some twisted circus. It was then that he decided to give up. There was no point in caring anymore. If he had any form of care for anyone before that point, which he did, he would now give it all up. He decided to strike one last time. This time it did not matter who he hurt. He was screaming out for attention. He wanted so bad to let someone know how bad he was hurting. He wanted someone to care.

It was late. It was probably 2:00 a.m. Raymond decided he was going to break into a pizza shop down the road in hopes of getting some drug money. His effort proved futile. He came away with eighty dollars' worth of coupons. His adrenaline was pumping now. The next night he broke into another pizza shop in town. This time he came away with less than three dollars.

He knew there would not be much money there. It was the same place he had worked at for three years. He knew the owner very well. He had become close friends with the guy while he worked there. He knew the owners' routine at closing time. In his mind, he wanted to jump the guy and take his cash drawer whenever he came out of the store. Raymond never had the guts to do such a thing as that.

Raymond didn't care that much about the money. To him, the thrill of the break-in was enough for him. His next place that he broke into was an auto mechanic shop. There he came away with three hundred dollars. He decided next to hit up his grandma's church. He got twenty dollars in coins before the sound of the janitor in the early morning hours spooked him.

Raymond knew that it was only a matter of time before he got caught. He already had a warrant out for his arrest. He had failed a drug screen that he had taken at a probation meeting. Raymond thought about skipping town. He had no money on him at the time however.

He paced the floor of the house he was in, trying to plan his next move. He knew that if the cops caught him, he was going to have to serve big jail time. He would possibly even be taken to prison. He rolled all these things over in his mind. How did it all come to this?

Suddenly, as if in a movie, he could hear police sirens outside. Two cop cars pulled up with their lights flashing wildly. He peered out the window. The police were walking up the steps to the apartment across the street where Raymond was supposed to have been staying. To his amazement, he had lucked out. They had the wrong house. A cop car sat right outside attempting to hide from detection if Raymond should happen to walk up to the apartment at any moment. His mind was racing so fast and he was nervous. His hands were shaking as he lit cigarette after cigarette.

He was four years old the last time he saw two police cars parked outside. They came and took him and his brother Jonathan away. Who was this person he had become? When he looked in the mirror he saw only evil. Here he was pacing the floor; the same scared four-year-old boy wondering what was going to happen next. He never meant for any of this to happen. It wasn't his fault he was sexually abused as a child, it wasn't his fault he was taken away to the orphanage, it wasn't his fault his mom abandoned him. It wasn't his fault that he never knew his real dad. It wasn't his fault!!

Anger burned within him. He seethed with hatred. How? Why? Where did it all go wrong? Why couldn't he have just been happy at the house with his new family? Why did his adoptive parents have to get divorced? Why couldn't he have just graduated from high school? He was so close before they finally had to kick him out. He was only two credits away. It wasn't supposed to happen this way. Raymond knew this was the end. In his mind, he would be in prison for a very long time. Yet, he had been in prison his whole life. He felt trapped. He hated the person he had become.

Somehow, and for some reason, Raymond was talked into turning himself in by a buddy of his who was in the house. He lit one final cigarette and with shaking legs he walked outside. He walked up to the policeman sitting in his car. The cop, shocked at first, rolled down his window. Then, with silent agreement, he stepped out of the car. He placed Raymond in the back seat of the vehicle. In one sense Raymond was relieved. The running was over. On the other hand, he was scared, unsure of what lay ahead. For now, he would take it in stride. He was not yet willing to give up. The hatred still burned within him.

He was taken to the police station and questioned for the recent string of burglaries. He denied any guilt. He said he had nothing to do with any of it. The police showed him a picture of a pair of shoes they found in the tan house. They were the shoes Raymond had worn on his first night of burglaries. He denied ownership. For now, they would lock him up for a probation violation until they could build a case against him.

Raymond sat in jail that night in utter hopelessness. Here he was in jail again. He was nineteen years old now and had been locked up four times, five if you count the time that he and his brothers got caught vandalizing cars in Ohio while on vacation. Boy was that a bad trip! Everyone shunned them for days. Raymond had it the worst because he was the one that turned them all in. That was way back when he was half-way decent.

Now, as he looked at himself, he saw only darkness. All the walls he had built up on the inside of him did not protect him at all. They ended up hurting him in the end. He would be going to court that next day to face all the charges against him. He knew he was guilty. Everyone knew he was guilty. Somehow, he thought he might get away with it. It was not likely, but he couldn't imagine being locked up for years and years. He wanted so bad to be free. But free from what was the question.

Even outside of these concrete walls he was still imprisoned. What did he have to look forward to? Nothing. He had a dismal existence to say the least. Still he had to try. The next day would be different. The lies continued to haunt him through the night. The blackness continued to linger over him; it was unwilling to relinquish its hold until it had destroyed its victim.

That next day on the way to court Raymond cursed God. He cursed the whole situation. He cursed life. He cursed his family. He cursed everything and everyone. Standing there in the elevator with his escort Raymond schemed. He thought of how he could jump this female guard and take her keys and gun. He thought of how he could escape. His mind raced but his body stood motionless. He could not even move. He was unable to act out this heinous plan.

Defeated for the time being, Raymond was escorted into the courtroom. There he sat with a stack of papers in front of him. The prosecutor and his probation officer sat across the room. Next to him sat Raymond's demons. The judge read off the charges that were being filed against him. There was a list of felony offenses. Raymond would fight it. He would show them. He would get out of all this. Somehow, he would fight it. Perhaps he could take it to trial. They had no real evidence on him. Yes, that's what he would do. He'd play the system that had played him out of his life.

The anger burned brighter inside of him as he was escorted back to the jailhouse. Darkness had fallen on Raymond. He was trapped. Every direction that he had attempted to turn to was blocked. The same darkness that had given him false hope and a false sense of security as a little boy was moving in on him to end his life once and for all. Who could save him now?

"Smaller"

I got my notepad out on my phone with the cracked screen
So many words in my head feels like a crime scene
God, help me put the words to these pages, this is my dream
Bringing glory to your name is what I what mean
I don't write to bring glory to me, that'd be stupid
If I want to be yours, I got to lose it
I'm not a loser, but I'm lucid
Aware of the life you died to give me, so I choose it
No more being bamboozled by the lies of the enemy
He's the loser, now move it
No more floozy, I'm choosy, I'm trusting In Him
That's the Christ, who is he?
Are you woozy? Turn up the speakers and don't snooze me
I'm skipping the chorus, so don't lose me...

STOP! REWIND...

I'm making war in the stars, I got my lightsaber
I'm making war in the bars, I got no paper
So addicted to drugs, I got no flavor, showing no taper
Getting high every night, I don't savor the labor
I'm married to lust and I hate her
If God is a game then I played her
If Jesus is a Lamb, then I flayed her
Do me a favor, call me a hater
Lights getting fader,
Tipping the scales, so full of myself
Where's the waiter? I slayed her

If sin is the bill, then I paid her
I need a savior?!
call me later...

Now, I don't know if you like me, I don't know if you're like me
But, if you're standing beside me, watch out for the lightning
Cause I'm lyin', I'm not a lion, I'm a liar
Like Pinocchio, my nose is getting longer

I used to be a baller! A shot caller!

I'm just playing with you,
I used to be smaller and smaller, wishing I was taller
So addicted to pain, I couldn't holler
Wishing I could color,
Outside the lines, but I was collared
Chain about my neck, while I wallowed
Lust and Lies on the menu while I swallowed
Heading off the cliff, but I followed
So much shame on the inside, I was hollow
Roasting on the fire like a marshmallow

Is it mollo or mallow? ....Yo, I was shallow!

Drowning in the deep of my sorrow
Wishing I could change, maybe Tomorrow, Tomorrow...
I couldn't love myself on the morrow
What's the matter with me?!!! Is what I hollered!
I studied sin like a scholar
I hated my Mom and I needed a Father
But I was farther and farther

So addicted to self, I was fodder
For the flames of Hell, getting hotter and hotter
The Devil used me like a martyr
I gave him my soul till I had nothing to barter
A powerless self-starter
So thirsty for love like a fish out water
You came into my cell and presented a charter
I signed on the line and now you're my Father!!!

By: Joshua Scott Zeitz

Above: One of the very few pictures of Raymond taken as an older teenager. Due to his many incarcerations and drug use he hated having his picture taken. The car was a favorite, belonging to his uncle in Freemont, Ohio.

7 "THE GREAT AWAKENING"

Meanwhile, a battle was being fought in the heavens over Raymond's soul. The prayers of his family and other saints were being launched to the throne room of God. One by one the creatures that had such control of Raymond's life began losing their grip. The darkness was dissipating. Raymond was about to be visited by a power that he had longed for his entire life.

The days passed by slowly. It seemed like a lifetime, yet it had only been two days. Raymond went and picked up a book from the cart in the front of the cell house. That night he read. The book told the story of a man who had also had a rough life. This man had been through much more than Raymond had. He robbed banks and did prison time. He was a big-time drug pusher.

Raymond read on as the book told of this man's childhood. He too had it rough when he was younger. Raymond somehow felt himself being portrayed on the pages before him. Suddenly it dawned on Raymond that he was not the only one who had struggled. Here was this man's story before him and yet there was something strangely wonderful about it all. The man spoke of a forgiveness that he had received through Jesus Christ.

He spoke of how this man Jesus had changed his life. He said that Jesus had died for his sins and that through faith in Him he was given a new heart and a right spirit. Raymond could not describe what he was feeling. Suddenly he felt a rush of wind come upon him. Raymond's mind raced back to the time that he had made that commitment back at the youth retreat with his mom and brother. He remembered the time he had faked like he was saved in jail. He remembered all the times he had cursed God. He remembered making fun of this man Jesus while he was high.

It all became so clear to Raymond. He was face to face with the reality of who he truly was. There was no one there to blame but himself. As if a movie was being played before his eyes, he saw all the evil atrocities that he had committed. Except this time, he did not feel sorry for himself. It was so weird. It was as if he was seeing things in an eternal perspective. He was seeing himself as the sinner that the man talked about in his book.

Raymond suddenly realized in that moment that he had sinned against God. He realized that he too needed this same Jesus to change him. A flood of emotions came upon him all at once. A still small voice was asking him if he wanted this same Jesus to forgive him and change him. Raymond could not hear the voice out loud. He just knew it was there. It was like there was someone else in that jail cell with him. Raymond instantly said yes, yes!

He began confessing all the sins he had committed. He remembered how he had made fun of Jesus. Raymond told Him he was sorry. Raymond's whole body was shaking. His body felt like it was on fire as tears streamed down his face. All the hurt, shame, anger, and hatred that Raymond had pent up inside of him all these years came tumbling out all at once. It was like someone was wiping him clean. He was being emptied and filled all at the same time.

It seemed like the whole ordeal went on for hours. Raymond had no idea what time the experience ended. But when he came to and looked around everyone was asleep. He was sure that if anyone had seen him during that time they probably thought he was a nut case. He didn't care.

For the first time in his life he was free. He felt no shame. A strange warmness and newness emanated from him. It was as if he was a new person altogether. He looked for that old feeling of hate, but it was gone! The demons fled in fear! The darkness was overwhelmed! Death lost its hold and a great light now shone bright upon Raymond! A smile that would light a room beamed across his face. He didn't know what just happened. All he knew was that he was free.

He felt a thousand pounds lighter. This same Jesus that had changed this hardened criminal in the book he read had just changed him. The same Jesus who was introduced to him by his adoptive mom had changed him. The same Jesus who Raymond had cursed and mocked had changed him. He could feel His love all around him.

A strange peace and joy flooded his very being. This was awesome. He could not stop smiling. He pulled the covers over his head. He leaped for joy inside. It was true!! All the prayers that his grandma and mom had poured over him; all the words of encouragement they tried to give him, it all made sense to him now.

He was seeing out of a different set of eyes. Instantly the things that used to appeal to him became abhorrent. He had no desire for drugs, pornography, cussing, hate, lying, and dirty thinking. They became his enemies. Strange new feelings of love crowded his brain. He wanted to tell someone, but whom? Everyone was sleeping. He was sure that everyone would probably think that he caught another case of jailhouse religion, but he didn't care. He would take it one step at a time. For now, he knew what had to be done...

*The picture **above** is the front cover of a card Joshua received from the Prison Chaplain after his baptism while incarcerated in 2003. A horse trough was brought into the recreation area for the baptismal pool!*

"Chasing Shadows"

"For what shall it profit a man, if he shall gain the whole world, and lose his own soul." ~ Mark 8:36 (KJV)

Microphone checka, hit me with that peppa,
Pulling out that sweata, so cold, so old, recall, unfold.
Sittin in that jail cell, no bail, so fail,
I see hell, it's so stale, please do tell.
See, I grew up in those suburbs,
So white, I get that sunburn.
That's me, latchkey, so high up in that backseat.
Yeah, I'm so cool, nah I'm so fool,
Got kicked out of that high school.
Now I'm no job n', I'm so slob n' and got no mob,
Now please stop it, but I can't drop it.
I'm so mad, I'm so bad,
I was so close, man, I coulda had it.
Story of my life, man, I'm so pathetic.
Couldn't cope with it, so I hit the attic.
Now I'm so high, and I can't cry,
been hittin' those drugs just to pacify.
I buried those hurts so deep inside
Man, I can't lie, I couldn't hide it.
So addicted to pain, I couldn't rectify it.
Now I'm so floored, and I hate the world.
I'm DNR, now the pull the cord.

I'm chasing shadows, and nothing matters.
I said I'm chasing shadows, and nothing matters,
nothing matters at all.
I'm chasing shadows, and nothing matters at all.
I'm chasing shadows, chasing shadows,
and nothing matters, at all.

Breathe in, breathe out.
You breathed life me in me,
but that's not what I'm about.
I'm a faker, I'm a taker,

Conceited, defeated, I'm heated, I'm bleeding,
I'm deep in the feed, and I'm feet in the deep,
and I'm reaping the life that I laid in the creep,
and I'm cheap, like a sheep that is lost in the seep,
My face in my hands, as I weep in the sink.
I hunger, I thirst, and I just need a drink
of that life, when you died on the cross, to give me.
My sin pierced your side, your hands, and your feet.
I'm crying out to you Lord, I just want to be free!!

I'm chasing shadows, and nothing matters.
I said I'm chasing shadows, and nothing matters,
nothing matters at all.
I'm chasing shadows, and nothing matters at all.
I'm chasing shadows, chasing shadows,
and nothing matters, at all.

You gave your life, your sacrifice, it shined a light
upon the night of my heart, it's so bright.
I shook away from your grace, but you said it's alright.
You hung there bleeding and dying, I relished the sight,
but you did it for me, and I didn't realize,
Oh God, please forgive me, I was wrong, not right
You wiped away my sin, you gave me new life!
No more chasing shadows, no more creeping at night!
I live in the light, live right, live tight.
I take up my cross, I lay down my life!
In hopes that one day, they'll see you're alright.

No more chasing shadows, cause my life matters,
because of you Lord, my life matters.
No more chasing shadows,
no more chasing shadows,
no more chasing shadows!
Because of you Lord, my life matters now.

By: Joshua Scott Zeitz

8 "A NEW BEGINNING"

Hope has a name: Jesus.

Over the next few days that passed, it seemed that all Raymond could do was read his Bible. It was like he was a sponge soaking up every word that came across the pages. He set up a meeting with the Chief of Police who had arrested him. There, in that meeting, Raymond confessed to all the crimes that he had committed. He tried to tell the cops how he got saved and how he just knew this was the right thing to do.

He was a little frightened at what would happen, but he felt a great peace after doing it. He called his family and told them what had happened. He wrote apology letters to all the people he had robbed. He wrote letters to many people telling them of his conversion. He would understand if they didn't know what to think at first. After all, he had done a lot of damage to a lot of people. He did not feel guilty however. Instead, by the grace of God, he prayed and read his Bible more and more.

For eight months, he studied the Word. There were times when he was tempted and tested in there, but by God's grace, he came out on the other side unstained and unspotted. God was continually teaching him how he had become a new creation, and how much God loved Him, and what great plans that he had for his life. There in jail, Raymond had the opportunity of leading others to Christ. It was there that he made new friends. He held Bible studies in his room. He even had communion with chips and juice.

Sure, some of the inmates mocked and ridiculed him. But he knew that he was just like that at one time. He prayed for them. He hoped that they too would come to know this Jesus that he was becoming increasingly fond of. There in jail, Raymond received his GED. That was an emotional day for him. That was the biggest thing he had ever accomplished in his whole life.

The months passed by quickly for Raymond. Through a miracle of God, he was not going to have to serve prison time. His lawyer worked out a huge plea bargain agreement with the judge, the prosecutor, and the probation officer. His grandma also wrote letters to the judge telling him of Raymond's conversion. Raymond also did the same. He even had the great privilege of telling the court himself the reason for his change.

As Raymond sat in jail those last few days of his sentence, he looked back at all that God had brought him out of. He thought about all that Jesus had forgiven him of. He was immensely grateful for this new-found relationship he had. He was reminded of the place in the Bible that says, *"When my father and my mother forsake me, then the LORD will take me up."* (Psalm 27:10 KJV) Raymond thought about how much resentment he used to hold in his heart against his mom and dad and even his adoptive parents. He thought about how much hate he used to have towards everyone in general.

Raymond could scarcely believe how God had transformed his life. To most people, if you were to tell them the story of how he was changed, they probably would not believe it. But for Raymond, it was as big a reality and truth than he had ever known. He could truly say with the songwriter, he once was lost but now he was found; he once was blind but now he could see.

It's funny, thought Raymond to himself; he never would have pictured anything like this happening to him. He never went looking for this to happen. Oh sure, he always had a longing in his heart for something more. He had a deep uneasiness and sadness that seemed to follow him wherever he went. But there was nothing that he could ever do that satisfied that longing in his heart. No matter how much dope he would smoke, or how much sexual perversion he practiced, at the end of the day he was always still so empty inside. All he had to show for it was more shame and more guilt.

Never in a million years could Raymond ever have gotten filled or completed by any of the things he used to do. Funnier still, to Raymond, was the thought that suddenly struck him, as he sat there awaiting his final release from jail. Never in a million years would he have ever been able to dream up such a god as Jesus.

He felt so blessed and loved at that moment. Jesus had rescued him from a lifetime of bondage and fear. Jesus Christ was his new Lord and Master. Jesus Christ was his savior. By God's mercy Raymond was visited in that jailhouse by the same Jesus whom he used to mock and ridicule. Jesus did not slap him or abuse him. He simply touched him. That touch caused the demons to flee instantly, and Raymond was no longer a hideous creature. He was a new creature in Christ Jesus! He was no longer Raymond Gann. He was now Joshua Zeitz!

As Joshua sat there pondering all these things he said a quick prayer. He prayed that wherever he went and whatever happened in the future, that Jesus would go with him and that this message would always burn bright within his heart. He prayed that one day he would be able to share his story just like the man in the book he read. And that someone somewhere just like him would also be changed by God's unfailing love.

> "Let the redeemed of
> the Lord say so,
> whom he hath redeemed from
> the hand of the enemy."
> ~Psalm 107:2 (KJV)

Joshua with his Mom, November 2017

"Without a doubt, Josh is the biggest miracle I've ever seen!" -Mom

"The ABCs of God's Grace"

Zapped by Grace – I'm changed!!!
Your love my new claim!
X out the old me, rearranged
Washed by your blood – no more stain!
Verily, verily I've been saved!
Under your Grace
Tied to your Ways
Stuck like adhesive I remain
Readily reading your Word
Quickened by the same
Past the pain
Over and over again
Nodding my head to your fame,
My heart's been swayed
Lust and lies are slain
Killing with kindness my thing!
Jesus my King!
I've been tamed
Hope is aflame
Grace is the power
Fanning the flames
Eroding the games
Drained of myself
Calling out to your Name!
Blown away by your grace!!
Addicted to Your love – No more Shame!!

   By: Joshua Scott Zeitz

*Joshua and his beautiful wife, Mitzi,
September 2017
Loving Life & Loving Jesus!*

"And all thy children shall be taught of the Lord; and great shall be the peace of thy children."
~Isaiah 54:13 (KJV)

A LETTER FROM THE AUTHOR:

Almost 15 years have passed since I was transformed in that jailhouse in Indiana and ever since then this book has been in the making. God has been so faithful to me! I am married to the most beautiful woman ever (14 years this November) and we have three awesome children! I remember looking in the mirror soon after I was transformed in that jail house and for the first time in my life I saw brightness and joy in my eyes that I had never seen before.

You may be wondering about the name change part where Raymond became Joshua – At Jack and Betty's house their youngest birth child was also named Josh so from that point on whilst living there, I took on the name of Raymond, which was my middle name.

I was born Joshua Raymond Gann, and after I was

adopted, I assumed the name Joshua again and changed my middle name to match my new adoptive dad's middle name – Hence my name from that point on was
Joshua Scott Zeitz!

However, even after the name change I still lived in the past – as that scared boy, Raymond. But then Jesus touched me, saved me, and transformed me and I was no longer stuck in the past. I truly began to walk in newness of life!

It's funny now to look back upon that boy I was in these pages, it's like I am writing about a person I used to know and honestly that is the case.

The Bible says in 2 Corinthians 5:17, *"Therefore if any man be in Christ, he is a new creature: old things are passed away; behold, all things are become new"* (KJV).

Upon giving my heart to Jesus, he did not simply give me a new lease on life or a new outlook on life, he gave me life. Up until that point I was dead inside. All I knew how to do was sin and live in darkness. I was hurting, alone, and ashamed. But thank God, he saved me!

During those months in jail there were times when that old darkness would try and creep back into my life. I had guys at one point that would walk by my cell and throw pornographic pictures inside or else they would leave them strewn about on my floor or bed while I was away at recreation.

They saw a change in me. They saw a light in me that they did not have and honestly it made them angry. People would call me names at times referring to me as a Bible-nut, and honestly <u>all these things simply confirmed the change that had taken place in me!</u>

Before when I had professed Christ in jail – simply giving lip service to try and fool God into letting me out –these things never happened. I never had guys calling me names or trying to tear me down or tempt me.

I wasn't changed. I didn't belong to God. I wasn't a

part of His family. Yet, after I truly said yes to Jesus, repented of my sins, and allowed him to change me according to His word, the Bible, I was adopted again – into *His* family and from that point on I got another new name and it was written in the Lamb's Book of Life in Heaven!

I now have a hope beyond this life. I now know with 100% absolution that I will live eternally with Jesus even after my life here on this earth ends.

I've had people through the years try and tell me that Jesus may work for me, but it's not really their thing. They may try and make a case for Atheism, or following some other god like Buddha or Allah. They may even say, "You know all it takes is a strong will power and you can make the positive changes needed."

This is my reply to that – I don't know about Buddha or Allah or any other god, all I know is that Jesus is the only one who died for me. He is the only one that was raised from the dead for me. Ultimately, He was the only one to visit me in that jail cell that day!

As for the will power part – Yes, it's true a strong will power can evoke some change in a person's life, but it has no power to forgive sin. It holds no power to transform a life, to give a person a new heart, to make them a new creation.

Perhaps you are reading this book and you have been trying to plug the holes in your life through various means – It may be religion, will-power, doing it in your own strength, perhaps you have chosen to use drugs, pornography, or other reality altering means to escape.

Whatever the case may be, I want to let you know that Jesus loves you! He died for you! He wants to give you life. He wants to heal you!

Scripture says, *"For God so loved the world, that he gave his one and only Son, that whoever believes in him should not perish, but have eternal life."* (John 3:16, WEB)

The very next verse says, *"For God didn't send his Son into the world to judge the world, but that the world should be saved through him."* (John 3:17, WEB)

Jesus is not here to make you feel bad about yourself. He doesn't want to hurt you or abuse you or embarrass you. He wants to heal your pain, to break the chains of addiction in your life; He wants to transform you into a new creation!

Will you let him? Will you say yes to Jesus and no to sin? If you want Jesus to change you, if you want to have a relationship with Him, if you don't know for certain where you will spend eternity – either in Heaven or in Hell – there is a way to know, his name is Jesus!

The Bible says, *"that if you will confess with your mouth that Jesus is Lord, and believe in your heart that God raised him from the dead, you will be saved."* (Romans 10:9, WEB)

If God is tugging at your heart right now and you want to say yes to Jesus, please follow this simple prayer to allow Him to come into your life and to transform you into a new creature:

Repeat this prayer – "Jesus, I believe that you died for my sins. I believe that you were raised from the dead. Forgive me for my sin. I accept your gift of salvation now. Come into my life. Come into my heart. Save me Jesus. Satan, sin, I turn my back on you, Jesus I turn to you now, save me, heal me, transform me. In your name I pray, Jesus, Amen."

Now begin to thank God for the work He has done in your life. Confess openly that Jesus is your Lord. I would encourage you to get a Bible if you don't already have one – read it. Find a good church, one that teaches the Word of God clearly and openly and begin to walk out this new relationship with Jesus!

My prayer for you is that God will show Himself mighty in your life. I pray that God will teach you to hear his voice, that He will speak to you through His

Word – the Bible. As you are faithful to read it, He will be faithful to help you understand it and live it out long and strong!

The Bible says in James 4:8, *"Draw near to God, and He will draw near to you…"* You can have a personal, intimate relationship with Him. It's not about offering Him lip service or trying to pull one over on Him, it's all about living life to the fullest through His strength not your own.

Thank you so much for reading this book. I pray that it has blessed your life and ultimately, I pray that you will come to know as I have for certain more and more about God's Unfailing Love!!!

Joshua Scott Zeitz

Above: This "Rags to Riches" picture is the original title and subtitle Joshua created for his testimony during his very last incarceration.

*The drawing **above** was one of many, many, drawings with scriptures that Joshua hung on the walls in his jail cell with toothpaste while he was incarcerated.*

note?

Letter from a "guide" -

Above all I am pleased that Joshua Zitz requested that I add to his ~~collection~~ painful and insightful recollections. Primarily because he really trusts someone who at pivotal tumultuous times in his young adult life tried to guide him away from his evil of wrongdoing legally. ~~I couldn't~~ At first observation of Josh's aura, he was void of life, love, ~~to~~ joy and trust. This young man would sit in my office looking at anything but my eyes. His ~~yickey~~ body ~~seemed to~~ attempted to muster energy to move through a dark life.

After many attempts to recommend he attend counselling, patch-up old grievances with family members, he found himself on many occasion being found guilty of theft to survive. He wondered aimlessly in desperation.

Unimaginably, happiness has overcome me over ~~the~~ last five years of "supervision". To actually witness his spiritual rebirth from

loneliness, shame, guilt, sorrow, and hurt has been overpowering. Josh is a true believer in Christ and his teachings. Little "Raymond" has proven time and again that he is a proud ~~father~~ new loving father and citizen of this world.

We now lock eyes in trust and admiration in knowing that his path to self-worth and love has ~~been~~ ~~to~~ healed.

Above: Original hand-written letter written by Jody Thompson, Joshua's probation officer.

Letter (Note) from a "Guide"

"Above all, I am pleased that Joshua Zeitz requested that I add to his raw and insightful recollections, primarily because he finally trusts someone who at pivotal tumultuous times in his young adult life tried to guide him away from his evil of wrongdoing legally. At first observation of Josh's aura, he was void of life, love, joy and trust. This young man would sit in my office looking at anything but my eyes. His gray lanky body attempted to muster energy to move through a dark life.

After many attempts to recommend he attend counseling, patch-up old grievances with family members, he found himself on many occasions being found guilty of theft to survive. He wondered aimlessly in desperation.

Unimaginably, happiness has overcome me over his last five years of "Supervision." To actually witness his spiritual rebirth from lowliness, shame, quiet sorrow and hurt has been overpowering.

Josh is a true believer in Christ and his teachings. Little "Raymond" has proven time and again that he is a proud and loving husband, father, and citizen of this world.

We now lock eyes in trust and admiration in knowing that his path to self-worth and love has been healed."

My daughter's (Moriah) personal interpretation of 2 Corinthians 5:17, drawn freehand.

Part II:
Joyfully Ever After

INTRO TO PART II

...And Joshua rode off into the sunset and lived happily ever after. Oh, how we wish sometimes life was like a fairytale or a cheesy romantic comedy, but it's not, and for me that's a good thing.

You see, God has designed each one of us to be unique creations and He has given each of us unique gifts, talents, abilities, and above all free wills to exercise these gifts, talents, and abilities.

I am so thankful to God for all that He has brought me out of, and all that He has brought me into.

In this Part II of Rags to Riches, *Joyfully Ever After*, Raymond is gone! I no longer have to hideaway behind a façade of toughness in an attempt to mask shame or guilt. If you notice, I am no longer writing in third person either, but rather in first person. This signifies the radical transformation that has occurred in my life! Yet, I've had to learn how to walk out this transformation long and strong. I've had to learn how to recognize God's voice, how to walk daily in relationship with Him, how to live out practically the principles that are put forth in the Word of God. Ultimately, I've had to learn how to be a Christian – to be like Jesus!

Therefore, I thought it favorable to write a little bit about my life after being radically transformed, after becoming a new creation (2 Corinthians 5:17).

Take a look at a marriage as an example: when a

couple gets married, although they may have dated for some time or been engaged for some time – it's an entirely different matter when you live in the same house, share the same bathroom, the same bed, wake up next to the same person, day after day.

All of a sudden, that same person who you once knew to have the most pleasant breath, hair, laugh, or clothes may not be so pleasant-like after day 200, let alone day 3! We have to learn how to love that other person no matter what their hair looks like in the morning. We have to learn how to love them in spite of their shortcomings. How much more then, do you think we need to learn how to love God – to truly get to know His character, to love Him in spite of what others say about Him, in spite of things not always going perfectly in our lives?

Herein lies a huge nugget of wisdom – God is not trying to take things from us, He is trying to get things to us! My Pastor, Pastor Jim, is always saying that God is not a cancer-causing car wrecking creator, but a loving, life giving Lord! How true that is! The Bible says in Hebrews 11:6, that whoever comes to God must believe that He is and that He is a rewarder of them that diligently seek Him. He is a rewarder! He is not some cosmic tyrant in the sky waiting for the first moment to strike us down. He is quite the opposite.

In fact, the Bible says in John 3:16-17 that God so loved us that He gave his only begotten Son. Then, in verse 17, it goes on to say that He sent his son into the world not to condemn the world, but that the world might be saved through Him! The marvelous thing about God and His love toward us is that we were condemned already but again the Bible says in Romans 5:8 that God commanded His love toward us in that while we were yet sinners, Christ died for us! That is a marvelous thing.

As you read about some of the things that have gone on in my life after accepting Jesus Christ as my Lord and Savior, please keep in mind that God is a good God and He loves you so much. I pray that you will open your hearts and minds to all that God wants to get to you and that you will learn to live as I have, joyfully ever after…

By: Joshua Scott Zeitz

Mitzi & Joshua in 2003, newly weds!

9 "HAPPILY EVER AFTER"

After being released from jail that final time, I was a new person! God had radically changed me in jail. I had the opportunity while incarcerated to lead others to Christ, to have Bible studies in my cell, to be baptized, to receive my GED, to make amends with many of my family members, to share my testimony with police officers, with court officials, with former friends – In essence however, I started not to mind jail as much. It was a comfort zone for me. I wouldn't say I became fully institutionalized, but I did come close. This oftentimes happens to individuals who spend much time incarcerated; they begin to like the safety of the concrete walls and the stringent structure and routine.

Upon release, I will admit that I was a bit scared as soon as that final metal door shut behind me. I was 19 years of age, soon to be 20 in a few months, and I had no place to live, and had I gone back to live in Fortville, I am not sure how I would have coped. I praise God for my dad who was wise enough and kind enough to pay for me to be sent to Richmond, Indiana where I would be enrolled into a Bible College/Work Program.

At the time however, I must admit that I was a bit angry and saddened because I was hoping to make amends with my dad and younger brother, be invited to come live with them –live happily ever after back at home reconciled, but now in hindsight I am sure that would have been a stupid thing to do and thankfully – although it was bittersweet because I didn't get a chance to talk to or see my dad, he knew it would be best that I not go back home.

My mom and grandma came to pick me up from jail, and that day they took me out to buy some new clothes – the ones I had on stunk pretty bad – they were the same clothes I had been arrested in 8 months prior! My dad had given them some money for that as well. As soon as I had some new clothes, we drove straightaway to Richmond, Indiana, about an hour drive, and after grabbing a bite to eat, they checked me into a hotel for the week, again paid for by my dad! I would stay there until I was able to get registered and fully checked into Bible College.

I was going to be working for the Lord and going to college at the same time, studying Pastoral Theology. On the outside looking in, everything was going to be A-Okay! After all, I was saved. I was born-again. I was a Christian – A Christ-One! I was on my way to living my happily ever after.

Yet, what I didn't know was that this was all going to take a lot of work and time and dedication and persistence and patience and diligence and let's face it, I was used to getting up to the sound of the door dropping on the food slot where I would then stand in line with 23 other inmates to get my state-issued oatmeal and juice that tasted more like soap, sit on the stainless steel bench and eat breakfast while reading the morning paper – I loved the little Billy Graham question and answer articles!

After breakfast, most everyone would go back to bed until they heard the food door drop again signifying it was time for lunch. For me however, this was my time to shine! I loved morning times in jail because many inmates after hording sleeping pills the night prior didn't even want to get out of bed in the morning. This meant that I would oftentimes get extra oatmeal and toast! The toast always had way too much butter on it and I would scoop the oatmeal which always had way too much brown sugar in it onto the toast with my little orange state-issued *spork* and eat, eat, eat until I couldn't eat anymore! I would then proceed to the front of the pod – (the name for the 24-man housing unit I lived in) and turn on the television to watch various television preachers. After that, I would slip out of my rubber state-issued sandals (A.K.A. shower shoes – trust me you don't want to take a shower without them) into my state-issued orange deck shoes which had so many holes in them that I had to stuff them with toilet paper for extra padding and then there was the smell so I would lace them heavily with baby powder every morning as well.

I would then walk the room. For like an hour or two or three I would simply walk in a big circle around the room, over and over and over again. While walking, I would oftentimes quote scriptures that I had been attempting to memorize. I would also think and pray and that was how I spent most every single morning for months.

After lunch time, I pretty much stayed in my cell, because this was when everyone else was finally awake and the pod would get really loud all the way up until lights out, and even after lights out most nights. During the day, the guys were always either playing poker, watching television, screaming and yelling mostly just for the sake of screaming and yelling. Recreation was one hour per day and this was when we would all be shuffled into the recreation yard, which was actually just a big room with two screens at the top of the ceiling where we would get sunlight if we were lucky. There were a couple basketball hoops and one or two basketballs that were always well worn and felt more like kick balls.

Sometimes we would have church or Bible study if enough volunteers made it into the jail and then only if the pod had behaved that day. Sometimes recreation time was really just an excuse for the officers to perform shakedowns on the cells looking for any contraband, drugs, or hooch (jailhouse alcohol).

Other than that, very little varied from day-to-day other than sometimes we would get new inmates or some inmates would get released. Fights would occur or some guy would decide that it was necessary to start screaming and yelling and get the guards to come into the pod or lock us down. This was jail, not prison, so there was very little to do in the way of activities and you didn't leave the pod or go outside ever unless you were a Trustee.

The little food slot would drop in the morning, and the whole process would start again – over and over again. You would be surprised however at how easily you adapt to this type of life. The main reason many guys or gals get into trouble while incarcerated, oftentimes it's because this routine gets messed up either by someone else's behavior, perhaps they ran out of oatmeal and had to serve grits, or one of the officers forgets to do something or privileges get taken away - whatever the reason, when this routine gets interrupted sometimes it causes high levels of stress and anxiety because inmates come to rely on these things.

So much power and control and dignity is stripped from you when you are locked up that having certain things happen at certain times is the only thing that brings stability and order into a person's life behind bars in many instances.

Now fast forward back to Bible College and here am I fresh out of this type of lifestyle, sitting in the office of the main Pastor and he is asking me all sorts of questions and making sure I have what it takes to complete the program, and so forth, and all I can do is naively shake my head and give him the best, most Christian answers I can muster.

After a bit of apprehension on his part, he reluctantly accepted me into the college and into the work/study program. What this program entailed was that I was going to be working on the campus – in the kitchen – for so many hours and my work was then going to pay for my schooling. All-in-all it was not a bad gig. However, I hadn't been to school since I was 17 and during that time, my senior year, I slept through most my classes, if I bothered to show for them at all.

There were times where I would literally receive a test – put my name on it, turn it in blank, go back to my seat and sleep until I heard the bell ring. Other times, I would stand up during the teacher's lecture and simply walk out of class and leave school or else I would sneak out to the parking lot for a cigarette. It finally got so bad, that after one of my smoke breaks one day the Vice Principal was waiting for me after I came back inside and he told me that they were kicking me out. My dad had tried his best to convince the school to keep me on, the Vice Principal even had tried to work with me on numerous occasions, but I simply couldn't and wouldn't cooperate and so a few credits shy of graduating, I was expelled from High School.

I earned my GED in jail and that was such an awesome experience! However, it was much easier to "go to school" in jail. Also, I was receiving good time (this is when you do certain things like get your GED, take a drug/alcohol program and upon completing these programs you shave a day off your sentence for every day you are in the program) so It was a major motivator as well.

Here, (at Bible college), I wasn't getting any "good time" and the only thing to keep me motivated was the idea of having some future after college and honestly, I had no idea what that even looked like! Before being radically transformed by Jesus, <u>I never thought I was going to live to be 20 years of age</u>. I lived so recklessly and care-free that I couldn't imagine living to be an adult or be married or have children or even be happy, ever – so this whole school and work thing was a huge shocker for me.

I mentioned that I had a job in part one, and I did. I got a job at a local pizza shop when I was 14 years old and I worked there for a few years. I did really well. My boss gave me a couple different raises and I learned a lot, but again I was a child so I was only allowed to work so many hours a night and only so many hours a week and all the money I received was mine alone. I had no bills, no responsibilities, nothing.

By the time I was 16 or 17 I had saved like $3,000 and even had investments in the local bank. However, after my drug addiction got so bad I actually went to the bank and withdrew all my money, threw it into the glove box of the Camaro I stole from my dad and had a guy drive me around to different parties and we smoked and drank all that money so fast I don't even know where it went. More than likely, although I can't prove it, but knowing the type of guy this was who I was hanging out with, he probably took it all after I was so wasted that I didn't even remember. Needless to say, I wasn't ready for college life or adult life for that matter!

I was at the Bible College for just a little bit of time before I began flirting with some of the girls there. Now mind you, I loved Jesus and I had no intention of doing anything that would hinder that relationship with him, but that's the thing, up to this point, I was pretty much self-taught if you will in the ways of the Bible and being a Christian. Everything I knew about being a Christian or about the Bible was via my own interpretations of it, or from what I heard from the various television preachers. I didn't have a Pastor or a mentor or anything like that. I wasn't discipled or taught. I was simply a guy who once was lost, but now found, once blind but now I saw, and can I tell you honestly that sometimes what I saw wasn't Jesus at all but other people, and <u>I began to find my identity in what others saw in me instead of who I was in Christ.</u>

The girls at the school there began showing me attention and I relished it. It's so crazy to say this and after reading about my life in part one, it might sound crazy to hear, but I was so naive. I was naïve to the fact that these girls were not really interested in me at all but they were using me for their own gain. You see they were high school students there, boarding school students – the ministry there served as a Bible College but its main focus and vision was a boarding school for troubled teenage boys and girls and so it gave the college students an opportunity for hands-on ministry while studying.

For me however, I had never really had a girlfriend. By the time I reached the age where most boys and girls start liking each other, I was already heavily involved in pornography and drugs so I was so ashamed of who I was that I never dared to ask a girl out or even talk to them for that matter. I used to laugh and say that my only girlfriend was Mary Jane (another name for marijuana). In all actuality, I hated myself so much that I could never see myself with someone so to be getting attention from these girls was something new and exciting.

These girls – one girl in particular – told me she was

17 and so in my mind, being 19, I was going to wait for her to turn 18 and we were going to fall in love and perhaps we would get married and I would graduate from Bible college...and again live happily ever after.

It may sound odd and cheesy and perhaps even a bit creepy, but this mindset was in me. Thank God that I got into a lot of trouble after the leadership found out that I had been writing letters to this girl and talking to her while she came through the food line and this little love thing or should I say fling didn't last long, even though my feelings were wrapped up in it all pretty good and I won't say it was easy to get away from.

In hindsight, I am so thankful that I didn't get any more involved with that girl or any of those girls for that matter because I later found out that they were just playing on my emotions and that was one of the main reasons they were sent to that boarding school in the first place – for being manipulative and I'm so thankful that I didn't do anything more stupid than writing notes!

Now fast-forward just a little bit after that and here I am working in the kitchen – and in she walks – a different girl this time! Thankfully this one is a college student. The head kitchen lady introduces us and tells me that this girl, Mitzi was her name, had just gotten back from a mission trip to Panama and I'm all like "Hey!" so dorky-like with my high socks and glasses on as I wave at her.

And that was it. She was gone and I went back to work and I didn't think much more of it. A bit more time passes and here I am sitting in class and who is it sitting next to me? Mitzi. I'm staring at her through my peripheral vision doing my best to pay attention to the lecture but also trying to get the full rundown of this new girl of my dreams without drawing any attention to myself.

Now fast forward just a bit longer and I'm in a car

with a buddy I met at Bible College there and we are driving down the hill toward the dorms and who do we see walking down the hill? Mitzi. She is walking all proud like down the hill – her arms swinging and the car stops! The guy driving, let's call him - Bob – rolls down the window and yells at her, "Hey, you want to go grab a bite to eat with us?" Little did I know that he had a thing for her and this was his attempt of wooing her.

To my amazement she said yes and gets in the car! I'm like "Hey," all dorky-like with my glasses. We go to McDonalds and while eating we are sitting next to each other, and she says, speaking to me, "Hey, look over there," I turn my head to look in the direction she is pointing and after turning about again, seeing nothing, I gave her a weird look and that look turns to an even weirder look as I realize that she has used this deceitful ploy as an opportunity to snatch my orange cream shake!

That night while sitting in Bob's house – he was trying to tell us all about his house and life and whatnot and the entire time this girl, Mitzi, and I are deadlocked – staring at each other. As we drive back to the dorms we are staring at each other the entire time. It was awkward but awesome. Her eyes were gorgeous and I was lost in them -those big brown pools! Neither of us could muster the courage to say much. At one point, I'm like, "Hey," all dorky-like with my glasses, "I, I-I, like your eyes."

That was it. I was hooked. We were hooked. We fell head over heels in love with one another. We stayed there at Bible College, both got our degrees. I became Pastor Josh and she became my wife and we had two and half children, lived in a big house with a white picket fence and lived happily ever after…

"Into the Light"

"For the wages of sin is death,
but the free gift of God is eternal life
in Christ Jesus our Lord." (Romans 6:23 WEB)

They say money makes the world go around,
and sex sells.
But what about the cell, the hell, the fell.
Oops, I mean the fall.
What about the walls that you throw up,
living in the dark with your hood up.
Hiding from the world, too ashamed to admit it.
You did it, you hid it, now you can't quit it.
It was fun for awhile, you were having a ball.
The lies took you in, man, you swallowed them all.

Look, I won't lie, it was great for a season.
Coughing and wheezing,
getting high every night for no reason.
Committing treason, lying and cheating.
But, now it's time to pay the piper,
Devil's got his sights set on me like a sniper.
Walls closing in, time is riper, living like a ciper.
Oops, I mean a caper.
I'm signed, sealed, delivered on this paper.

Whether it's adultery, sodomy, or pornography,
I need a lobotomy.
This lust and these lies, man, they're robbing me.
Living on the trash heap, it's rotting me.
Little by little, I'm dwindling, I've been swindling.
Praying every night to the ceiling, the cell in me,
has me trapped, and I'm sick in the head,
it's so ill in me.

I try to stop, but I can't, it's debilitating, so overrated.
These pleasure sensations are tainted.
I'm jaded, I'm faded, I hate it, I'm weighted,
I want to be free, just want to erase it.
But, I can't escape it, I'm trapped, the lies are evasive.
I'm stuck like adhesive, it's bleeding me.
Light up my life Lord, shine deep in me!

Like a fish out of water, I'm flailing.
At first, it was smooth sailing, no end in sight.
No mention of repercussions, no mention of light.
Did I mention repercussions?
Did I mention my sight?
Cause I'm blinded!
Creeping in the dark, chasing that first high,
I can't find it.
These repercussions are weighing heavily,
like a truck on my chest, I can barely breathe.
Jesus help me please, I need to see!
These demons won't leave me be.
I know I messed up, the lies and the lusting,
I confess them before you,
I can't handle these repercussions.
Lord please forgive me,
I was wrong, not right,
I want to walk in your light!

Once lost, but now I got sight!
Once addicted, but now I'm alright!
Your word resonates in my heart, like a drum,
and I'm loving it!
I've been freed from the lies, no more lusting it!
Did I mention Jesus saved me?
He's the master percussionist!

By: Joshua Scott Zeitz

10 "MITZI"

Okay, moment of truth...did you really think we rode off into the sunset and lived happily ever after? I mean the big house, the picket fence yeah, but the two and a half children? Come on, how is that even possible?

The truth of the matter is I was smitten with Mitzi! In fact, I was infatuated with her. I know in the movies they say its love at first sight, but for me it was more like lust at first sight. I mean this girl was beautiful! Again, I know, I was in Bible College and thank God, I wasn't studying to be a priest because I couldn't keep my eyes off of her. She was gorgeous.

She was 4'11" long brown hair, big brown eyes, and dare I say it, she had it going on in the body department. Can you tell? I was smitten.

Now the policy at the school – and rightly so – was that college students were not allowed to date. They wanted the students to focus on their studies, namely, on the Lord before pursuing things like relationships. However, to say that we did everything the opposite of what they wanted, would be an understatement. Not only did we "date," we just delved head long into the deep end of the pool. I mean there wasn't any wading in or testing the water –we went from me, all dorky like in my glasses saying "Hey," to making out in the Wal-Mart parking lot while everyone else was inside shopping.

For the sake of time and also to keep this book from becoming one of those cheesy romance novels you see in the library – you know the ones – with the barrel-chested man who has more hair than is naturally possible holding the scantily clad damsel in distress with one giant arm – long story short, we did it ALL wrong baby!

Please keep in mind that I was fresh out of jail and the only "relationship" I'd ever had up to this point in my life was in like 5th grade to a girl named Molly. She had one of her girlfriends call me up on the phone to ask me out and I said yes. The conversation was more just a bunch of giggles on their end of the phone and silence on mine, because I had zero idea what "going out" even meant.

The next day at school, I cussed the girl out and refused to talk to her again. Looking back, I know it broke the girl's heart but at the time, I didn't care. All I knew back then was that I wanted to look cool. You see the girl that had asked me out wasn't very "popular" and honestly, I thought the girl who had actually called me, Karey - liked me, but she didn't and so I didn't want to be seen with the unpopular girl so I guess you can say I dumped her, but in reality, I was just a jerk.

That's pretty much how all my girl interactions went from that point on. There was another girl, Jamie, she used to have such a crush on me. She would swoon over me all day during recess, chasing me around, writing me love letters. She even sent me a love letter to my house one time. I was so mean to this girl and I can remember feeling pricked in my heart because of it too, but I pushed the feelings aside in favor of looking cool and making people laugh.

It wasn't the usual girl hits boy or boy hits girl

because they really like each other type of thing. I was just cruel. One day in class, she went to sit in her chair, and I kicked it out from under her. She hit the ground so hard I could see in her face she was hurt, but again I pretended not to be bothered by it.

There was one girl in particular however that I really had a crush on, Ashley, and man-oh-man did I ever have a crush on her. If you remember back in part one, I told of how I used to rock in bed…Well at this point in my life I still did this and truth be told I still rocked in bed all the way up into the first years of marriage but now I'm getting ahead of myself. Spoiler Alert! Anyhow, I used to rock in bed at night and just chant non-stop – "I love Ashley, I love Ashley, I love Ashley." I would do this for long periods of time. I would say her name - Ashley Zeitz - to see how it rolled off my tongue. We did "go out" for a spell but she wound up breaking my heart after she dumped me.

During all this time – elementary school into middle school and into high school, I never was taught about relationships – about what it meant to date, to have a girlfriend, to be "in love." I was never taught about sex or about girls or the changes that occur in the body. The only sex education I ever received was in school when they would separate the boys and girls and show us weird videos about the birds and the bees and nature and honestly, I never had any clue what they were talking about most of the time.

Keep in mind, I had started experimenting sexually when I was six years old with little Amanda under the bed at the foster home and not to mention I was sexually abused by big Amanda as well. I had already had some experience with "sex," but I still didn't really know what it was.

I remember one time we had some ladies come in to talk to our class about the male and female body – this was when they first started hammering the whole idea of safe sex and using protection. I was 13 years old! I still had no idea what sex was and here were these ladies – grown women – coming into our middle school and telling us students how to practice it safely.

I remember them asking a question: "How can we practice safe sex?" No one in the room dared to raise their hand. I mean this was a class full of children. Somehow, I mustered enough courage to raise mine and I shyly answered, "Why not just do it with your clothes on." Everyone laughed and even the instructors laughed. You see even though I had played sex when I was younger and had been exposed to sexual things like movies and molestation, I was naïve to what it really meant to be intimate with a partner and rightly so – again I was only 13 years old.

What I was really trying to say at the time was, "Why do we need to get naked at all? Why can't we just show each other love with our clothes on?" Needless to say, I was embarrassed, and at the time, I laughed it off, chalking it up to me just making a joke. On the inside however, I was hurting and I hated making myself vulnerable like that.

Fast forward back to Bible college now and here I am face to face with a girl – a person of the opposite sex who actually likes me, and even though I was born-again at this point in my life, I had zero knowledge of what all these feelings I was having meant or what I should do with them for that matter, and so we both did what any other ignorant hormonally enraged young person would do, we just acted first and thought later and sometimes I didn't even think later – I just acted again.

A month or so passed and I turned 20 years of age. Mitzi was 19. She came to me one evening and said, "Hey, why don't we run away together?" I, being the holy pastoral theology student, who loved God and wanted nothing more than to serve Him and do His will, said "Okay, let's do it."

Would you believe it, I called a buddy of mine that I had met in jail, and asked if he wouldn't mind coming to pick me up. He lived about an hour away in Fishers, Indiana. That night, Mitzi snuck back into her dorm, packed a bag and I did the same. We met out behind her place and then proceeded to walk across the adjoining field to the fuel station to await our ride. We had no earthly idea what we were doing, where we were going, nothing. We just did it because we loved each other and this whole Bible college thing and the people there were just trying to keep us down. They didn't want us to be happy. They didn't understand the feelings we were having and so we would prove to them, ourselves, our parents, to God that we were in fact meant to be together and so that very night, we left.

Mitzi was the best thing that had ever happened to me. She was smart, beautiful, she loved God. She too had had a tough childhood. She was adopted from Panama and moved to Madison, Wisconsin. Now if that isn't a change – both geographically and climatically, I don't know what is!

Back in Panama, she had undergone physical and sexual abuse and after moving to the states, as she got older, she dealt with much self-esteem issues. She used to lie a lot to her adoptive mom – she didn't have a dad, he died shortly before she was adopted. She was rebellious and really didn't want to listen to her mom. She too knew little about the world or relationships and she certainly didn't grow up in a godly home.

At 16 years of age, her mom placed her at the boarding school there in Richmond and it was there she remained until the night that we ran off together, save for visits home and also the mission trip she went on. You can imagine that she was ready to get away from that place. She was ready to live her life.

About six months after coming to the boarding school, after a play called Heaven's gates, Hell's Flames, she gave her life to the Lord. She was born-again! She climbed the ranks in the boarding school – they had a level system where if you did right you were given more privileges. She did right, and she was close with the head Pastor there and she and some other girls would always go on outreach trips with the Pastor, travelling to various churches to talk about the ministry, share testimonies, and to also raise support.

She was also on the praise team. She loved to sing and needless to say here I was fresh out of jail and to everyone else looking in, I was there as an agent of the enemy – to take her eyes off of her calling, her purpose, and her God-given destiny. No one taught us how to do it right however. I mean they tried to come to us after the fact, but by then it was too late – we were smitten and that was that.

We were so naïve and immature and dare I say, we were just plain ignorant. We had zero clue of what it meant to be in a relationship, but we had these feelings of love for one another and for us that was enough – in our minds we were going to live happily ever after – in my mind I had what I had always dreamed of – a real relationship with a girl, Mitzi...

11 "ON THE MOVE"

After leaving Bible College, Mitzi and I stayed with the same buddy of mine that had picked us up for a few days. We slept on his floor upstairs, after that, we moved into another buddy's house (again whom I had met in jail) for one day. Then after that we moved into this buddy's mom's house. Her name was Irene. This was a God-send for us because we had zero money, no car, no job, nothing.

Irene was a hoot! Sometimes she would start singing out of nowhere. One time she even put an old record on and started dancing and swaying around the pole in the living room as if she was living some past memory. Then there were other times where she would wake us up in the morning, banging on our door, screaming at us to go out and find a job. She was quite lively, but lovely as well. She bought us lots of food.

Before I met Mitzi, when I was far younger, my dad taught me and my brothers how to cook. We would make big, extravagant meals for guests from church and for family members. He used to make us big breakfasts as well. Whenever we would have a friend sleep over, he would wake us up with eggs, hash-browns, cinnamon rolls, orange juice, toast and chocolate milk. He taught us how to make things like cakes, meatloaf, spaghetti and chili.

While staying at Irene's house I would make Mitzi sausage, eggs, and toast every morning for breakfast. I also introduced her to frozen chocolate pie with dream whip for her first time as well. Before me met, her entire diet consisted of hot Cheetos and personal pan pizzas from the gas station across the way from the school. Growing up, her mom made her eat salad for every meal and other than that they ate what came from the microwave – so her culinary world was blown wide open after meeting me.

We walked everywhere while staying with Irene. We were supposed to be "looking" for a job, but had no real intention of doing anything of the sort. For now, we were content just living our simple lives. It was like an extended honeymoon without the wedding or the marriage.

Needless to say, however, the honeymoon ended and Irene finally had to tell us to move because we were literally eating her out of house and home.

By this time, Mitzi and I were beginning to realize that life was not so simple and the reality of what we had done – her leaving the same place that had basically raised her from her teenage years and had given her opportunities to serve the Lord through music, college, and ministry and me – who had been radically transformed in jail, been given a fresh start in a new place, completely paid for – the reality of our sin was sinking in but we had no idea what to do next.

To this day, I still believe it was God's grace and mercy that kept us through this entire process of moving around and in our ignorance – our immaturity, it was God who watched over us and sent people into our life to help us. I can't say enough how thankful I am to Him and to those in our life at that time who helped us, gave us a place to stay, and showed the love of God to us even when we didn't deserve it at all.

I called my grandma after moving from Irene's home and she gave us a ride to a homeless shelter in Greenfield, Indiana that offered room and board for people without homes while they were looking for work or simply needed to get back on their feet. My grandma wasn't ready to have us stay with her. Granted I was a Christian now, but the last time I had stayed with her a few years back, I had shot her dog, had her phone shut off, and was hooked heavily on drugs so I can imagine her apprehension even now and especially since Mitzi and I weren't even married.

Upon taking us to the shelter however, we found out that we weren't going to be able to live together since we weren't a married couple. My grandma talked with us both and told us about the Bible verses that talk about marrying in favor of burning with lust and so forth and given the added pressure at the thought of being apart from one another, we decided it was best to heed her advice. That same day, November 21, she drove us to the mayor's office in Greenfield and we were married in his office with my grandma as the witness.

We walked back to her van in the parking lot, our marriage license in-hand, and Mitzi said to my grandma, "What have I done?"

Since we were now a legal couple in the eyes of the law, we were allowed to live in a family unit in the shelter and we stayed there for 90 days, which is the maximum allotted time. While there, Mitzi and I got a job delivering newspapers. We had to get up every morning and fold the papers, stuff them in a cloth poncho I wore with papers in front and behind. Sunday mornings were the worst because of all the advertisements. The papers were so hard to roll and then you had to stuff them into little plastic sheaths and this was no easy task. Mitzi was a champ through it all and there were times where she actually did the route for me cause let's face it, I was too lazy!

In early December, the 9th, Mitzi and I got married again – this time with more of a formal wedding. She wore a red dress – She looked absolutely amazing!! I wore a suit and tie. We were married by a minister who I had met in jail – he used to come in from time to time and conduct Bible studies for the inmates.

My grandma and mom came, my dad came – they were divorced by now. Mitzi's best friend from Bible College, Lisa, came. My best friend from Bible College, Maurice, came – he was my best man. My grandparents from Ohio were there. Miss Martha, a sweet lady from the school was there, she played the piano while Mitzi sang to me. I cried the entire time!

It was an awesome experience and to have friends and family there, even though our circumstances weren't the greatest, meant a lot to us. It made me feel validated in a way – It gave me hope for the future, even though I had no clue what that future held.

It was nearing winter time now and we found out that Mitzi was pregnant! We were going to be having a baby! It all happened so fast. Just a few months prior I was introduced to this pretty little lady and now here we were living in a homeless shelter and pregnant?! I had no idea how to be a dad, but I will say this: not one time did we ever think about abortion or regret being pregnant. In fact, we loved the idea. We had no idea what we were doing, but we were so excited.

Winter came and with it came the snow. I remember one evening in particular, Mitzi was having mega cravings for a cheeseburger and we were a mile away from any cheeseburger, we had no car, there was a blizzard outside, we weren't allowed to leave the shelter after a certain time, and that certain time was now!

Anyhow, I decided that I was going to brave the storm and the shelter's rules in favor of getting my now-pregnant wife a cheeseburger. I climbed out the window and walked the mile or so down the road in the blaring white snow to Burger King to get Mitzi a whopper. I got back and Mitzi let me in the back door.

Let's just say that some of the people there at the shelter didn't care for us too much. Not only were we far too carefree for our circumstances, but we only had a paper route as a job and that paid like nothing, and also for that Christmas, we were blessed by some people who came to visit the shelter with loads of Christmas presents like a television, a VCR (a thing that plays tapes, can you believe it?), pots and pans and gifts cards – some of the other families I think were a bit jealous of us, but we kept our heads high and chugged on.

Our 90 days were up and we were forced to move again. We had no idea where to go. A family from our small church at the time took us in. We had started going to this little church in Greenfield my mom had told us about and while there we met a couple really nice families. They let us stay in their attic. They had two small children who were the cutest things ever and we really loved spending time with them and getting to know them. We lived there for about a month and again got a job delivering newspapers.

After we moved from there, another family from the same church took us in and we lived in their basement. We no longer had the job with the newspaper and Mitzi was getting really pregnant now – she was due to have her baby in just a few months.

The man of the home there really encouraged me to find a job and to care for Mitzi. It was weird because he pulled me out of the house one night and had a talk with me on the front porch and basically told me man to man that I needed to step it up and love Mitzi more. I remember feeling kind of hurt by his words – no one had ever talked to me like that before, but it did open my eyes and I respected him so much for what he told me.

I found a job at a pizza place in the neighboring town. It was a perfect job for me because I had experience in pizza from my teenage years. Keep in mind that during this time, all I had was a GED and a felony criminal record. I had no work experience except for my job as a teenager and businesses are very wary of hiring anyone with a criminal record, let alone with felonies. So, this was quite a blessing to have this job. Not only that, but I was meant to run the place on my own at night. I made some pretty amazing pizzas during this time.

Since the job was in a neighboring town, I had to get a ride to work. Well, one night Mitzi and I were walking the neighborhood there and we passed a car that I really liked and it sparked the desire in me to pray for a car. We prayed for a car that evening, specifically for a Lincoln (Lincoln's have always held a special place in my heart because my grandpa had one when I was younger). The man of the home, where we were staying, traded in his 1969 Ford Galaxy that he had been renovating and working on for a Lincoln Continental and it was in the drive waiting for us the next day!

I hadn't driven a car since before I was incarcerated over two years prior and Mitzi had never really driven at all. It was such a huge blessing to us and we were so grateful.

You know, God is so good. Even when we don't deserve it, He is good. Even when we aren't good, He is so good. Just ten months prior I was 19 years of age and freshly released from jail. In that short span of time, Mitzi and I had run away from Bible college, lived in sin, got married, got pregnant, moved 6 times, lived in an attic, a basement, a spare bedroom, a homeless shelter and through it all God was there ready and willing to bless us, to take care of us, to have a relationship with us.

He didn't cause us to do any of those things. He didn't make us leave college to teach us something. He didn't put us in a homeless shelter. We did all those things and yet in spite of all those things he provided that homeless shelter for us to live in, those people for us to live with, that car, the pizza job, and so forth. In spite of us, He is always good and is always so willing to get things to us. It was our stupidity that took us away from His best for us. It was our sin that separated us from Him. BUT it was His grace that made a way. It was His love that provided for us. It was His mercy that spared us.

It came time to move on. We were going back to Bible College – back to what we believed at the time was our God-given destiny. I remember thinking at the time that this was it. We had finally learned how to live. This was our seventh move since leaving in the first place and the number seven is the number of completion. In my mind, it was finished. I was finally ready to be the man that God called me to be. Thank God for 2nd chances and for 10th chances – we were going back, we were on the move...

Mitzi & Joshua in 2010

12 "BACK TO REALITY"

Mitzi and I were so excited to be moving back to the place where we first met. We were moved into a home just off campus and to us this was a huge thing. Up to this point we had only lived with other people and honestly, we felt like this new move provided us again, with some validation, from our family members who up to this point saw us as quite immature. Now we had a house with a yard and I was going to be working on campus again as a janitor and going back to school. Mitzi was very pregnant by now – only a couple months away from giving birth, but they still wanted her to work as well, so she was given a job as a receptionist in the main office.

Everything seemed to be going okay and then we got news that they were moving us out of that house and onto campus. We would now be living in an upstairs apartment right above where the boys' basketball team lived. Gone was our house and yard, but we still tried to remain positive because after all we were in full-time ministry and these were simply sacrifices that needed to be made.

The new apartment was nice enough, although it was located right in the heart of campus and it could get pretty noisy downstairs. Plus, there were only three windows in the whole place one of which was a really tiny one located in what would be my office and the other two were in the far back of the two bedrooms. The ceilings in the bedrooms were slanted so I had to be careful not to bump my head (of which I did on some occasions). Mitzi of course had no problem with this being she stood 4'11" – 5' if you ask her. ☺

Trying to look on the positive side of things, I counted this as an 8th move and since 8 is the number of new beginnings, I counted this all joy! Can you tell? I was quite spiritual at this point in my life – although oftentimes my "spirituality" far outweighed my wisdom and/or understanding of life and reality.

I think it's important to remember again that Mitzi and I were still very much newlyweds and neither of us had any idea of the ramifications of full-time ministry life nor the amount of work that was involved.

Needless to say, I started to fall behind on my studies a bit and the new job as janitor was a lot of work. I was basically responsible for cleaning the entire school building – all the classrooms, the bathrooms, sweeping the floors, mopping, I was also charged with cleaning the church – vacuuming the sanctuary, cleaning all the classrooms, and I worked alone in the evenings.

This made it especially difficult because Mitzi was finished with work by 5 pm and yet I was expected to work into the evening and go to school in the mornings. Therefore, we rarely saw much of each other and when we did it was only for a little bit of time.

Again, I tried to remain positive telling myself that I was serving the Lord and that I was being a servant. In truth, I was being a servant in duty, but my heart was growing calloused because I was beginning to get burnt out. It was lonely working because everyone else on campus, the students, the teachers, the leadership, Mitzi were done working for the day and they all went home, whereas I was left to be the cleanup guy if you will and this began to take its toll on me.

The time finally came for Mitzi to have a baby and what an awesome experience it was! It was early morning and she had just gotten off the phone with my aunt when I walked into the room. As soon as I walked in, she hopped up off the couch and bam! Her water broke right there in front of me.!

To her surprise and mine if truth be told, I didn't freak out. I helped her to the bathroom where she took a quick shower while I made a few phone calls notifying family and the doctor of what had happened. Mitzi's mother happened to be in town visiting as well, so she was able to be there for the whole process which was a big blessing to her and Mitzi.

We had a bit of trouble at the hospital because Mitzi was not able to give birth naturally – something to do with her tiny frame – but the doctor was quite rude about the entire thing, saying at one point even that she sounded like one of his dogs! Can you believe it? Mitzi's mom was mortified and threatened to sue.

Push came to shove (no pun intended), Mitzi ended up delivering our first child, *Moriah Rachel Zeitz* on August 28th via a C-section.

It was a glorious moment and I was able to stand there and watch the whole process. It was crazy to witness the sights and sounds of the operating room with the doctors all talking about this and that like it was no big deal. I held Mitzi's hand most of the time and with the other I tried to catch it all on film.

Afterwards, I was able to help bathe Moriah for her first time and it was such a neat and emotional experience.

We were parents! I remember Mitzi was smiling from ear to ear. Her eyes were all watery and squinty and her cheeks were a bit red and she looked tired from such an exhausting experience mixed with the medicine, but she was so utterly happy.

We were able to stay in the hospital for a few days and we were so spoiled we never wanted to leave! The hospital wasn't too busy at that time, and so I was able to stay in the room with Mitzi and sleep on the adjoining hospital bed. It had raise and lower controls and a pull-out television which could be pulled right in front of your face. And then there were the all-you-can-eat mini ice creams in the community fridge just down the hall and the mini Sprites.

Mitzi was having a blast as well. She was learning how to breast-feed Moriah for the first time and the nurses were all so friendly. They came in all the time, attending to her every need and then if we wanted to sleep, the nurses would take Moriah back to the nursery. This went on for three full days and we loved it!

In a single moment, reality came rushing in and it was time for us to leave the hospital where we would be taking Moriah back to our upstairs apartment – above the boys' basketball team and I would be going back to serve the Lord as the janitor and after a few short weeks, Mitzi would be going back to work in the office where she would have to come home every day on her break and pump breast milk for the baby and life would go on – back to reality.

The months went by so fast. We loved watching Moriah grow. It was difficult at first adjusting to her crying, especially at night, but Mitzi did an amazing job through it all. She was a first-time working mom and she never complained. She was truly awesome and managed to breast-feed Moriah for nine full months – all the way up until we got pregnant again.

I remember coming home one time, before Moriah was born, and Mitzi was up on a step stool painting what would be Moriah's room - all pink. She had paint on her shirt, her hair, but a huge smile on her face. She was so excited to be having a baby girl.

We made the most of life in that upstairs apartment, but slowly our way of life began to take its toll. By now, I had fallen so far behind in school that there was no way I was going to be able to pass my classes. This was a requirement in order to live on campus and continue to be a part of the work/study program.

To make matters worse, they gave me a job as a counselor in the dorm as well and here I was responsible for third shift where I would have to do rounds every so often to check on the residents there who were asleep at this time. Unfortunately, I had a difficult time staying awake myself. Many nights, I would go into the back office and crash on the couch.

In the mornings was class and here I enjoyed the lectures very much – I loved learning about the Bible and the teachings of Christ, but I wasn't able to keep up with the homework at all. As a janitor, I began slacking as well and longing rather to be home with Mitzi and Moriah, I half-heartedly did my job and I would lie on my timecard, writing down hours that I worked that I really didn't work at all.

I loved God and I loved the idea of serving Him, but I was slowly drifting away from the purpose of it all. I was burnt out and I had no one to help me grow as a Christian. On the outside, I was a new dad, young, in love and quite "spiritual" even. I went to prayer every morning, where I would pray alongside the staff and Pastors and I would read my Bible and during church services, I would praise God and worship Him mightily, but on the inside, I was hurting. I struggled with my identity, with who I was in Christ, and I began to allow thoughts of me as a bad person to creep in and I saw myself as inferior next to the other spiritual giants that worked there – the other Pastors, the leadership, the other college students.

Behind closed doors – an old demon came back to haunt me, a demon I hadn't dealt with for some time; lust. <u>I began to act outwardly who I was on the inside or at least who I saw myself as</u> and I began to delve into pornography once again.

Here, within my own private quarters, I found solace. I allowed the enemy to bombard my mind with doubt, with depressing thoughts and I swallowed the lies he fed me. Slowly, I was drifting away from God, away from my relationship with Him, with Mitzi, with reality.

I wanted so bad to be free – to be a spiritual leader, to be someone God could trust, but instead I had succumbed to sin and adding to that I was lying on my time card, skipping out on class, on work and ultimately, I was heading off a cliff spiritually.

God is so gracious. His mercies are new every morning! I remember sweeping the floor one day in the school stairwell and the presence of God came on me so strong that all I could do was stop sweeping and just cry. I wept and wept and I could hear God telling me how much He loved me and what great plans He had for my life. I thought of the scripture verse in Jeremiah 29:11 where it says, *"For I know the thoughts that I think toward you, saith the Lord, thoughts of peace, and not of evil, to give you an expected end."* (KJV)

I knew at that moment that God still loved me, that He wasn't mad at me. He was waiting on me to come back to Him, to repent and to run into His loving arms so that I could begin to walk in His blessing for my life.

I went and told the assistant Pastor what I had been doing – lying on my timecard and I assured him that I was going to do better. Mitzi and I even underwent counseling of sorts to help our marriage that was hurting a bit by now because of all the mess that I had allowed into my life and into our home. We tried to fix what was broken, but it all came too little, too late and not long after, the leadership there asked Mitzi and me to leave.

Mitzi was pregnant again by this time and we would be having a boy! However, the circumstances surrounding this pregnancy were much grimmer and life was much more complicated.

Here we were again leaving Bible College for the second time and again not on good terms. Yet, we were determined to trudge forward and make the most of it.

I knew that God loved me and that He had a great purpose and plan for us, I just didn't know what. For now, we would just have to go out and try to find out what it was – our dreams of full-time ministry were dashed, for now it was back to reality…

Moriah Rachel Zeitz

"Put Him First"

"But seek ye first the kingdom of God, and his righteousness; and all these things shall be added unto you." ~ Matthew 6:33

Put Him First, Put Him First, Put Him First
Put Him First, Put Him First, Put Him First
I gotta, gotta, gotta Put Him First
Put Him First, Put Him First...

I'm in the lurch, getting high behind the church
Uncle's inside spitting Bible verses
I'm on the outside spitting curses
Highway to Hell and I'm the first
I'm driving the hearse!
I'm the worst, So perversive
I don't dabble in sin; I'm submersed, immersed in it
Like 24-7, I'm working it, rehearsing it
If sin is a sickness then I'm nursing it
If Jesus is light I'm inversing it
In case you don't know that's reversing it
If darkness is a place I'm traversing it
I need someone to save me that's subverting it
I need to rewind that's reverting it
Jesus save me please!
I'm conversing it, confessing it
Jesus be my Lord!
That's converting it, respecting it...

Put Him First, Put Him First, Put Him First
Put Him First, Put Him First, Put Him First
I Gotta, gotta, gotta Put Him First
Put Him First, Put Him First...

I gotta put Him first in these verses
Bringing glory to His name in the churches
I used to be the worst spitting curses
Now I tow a tight line keeping it terse as I worship
I don't have to, I get to
No more flirting with Sin cause He saved me
No more hurting, no more skirting from His Grace, He forgave me
Out of the dirt yo He raised me!
Goodness and Mercy it chases me!
End of the pencil erasing me
More of Him in my life replacing me
Jesus on the throne displacing me
Jesus in my life gracing me
With His presence - Like an artist He's tracing me
A Master Teacher He's training me
Never leaving nor forsaking me
So Captivated by His love!!!
Yo, He's taken me!!!

Put Him First, Put Him First, Put Him First
Put Him First, Put Him First, Put Him First
I gotta, gotta, gotta Put Him First
Put Him First, Put Him First...

I gotta, gotta, gotta, Put Him First!

By: Joshua Scott Zeitz

13 "A FRESH START"

"I called upon the Lord in distress: the Lord answered me, and set me in a large place." ~Psalm 118:5 KJV

In the previous chapter, I had mentioned how God spoke to me and comforted me in a trying time in my life and I want you to know that's just who God is! I was living in sin at the time and I wasn't exactly the most perfect husband or dad, but God didn't look at all that and simply give up on me. Instead, He kept trying to get to me His message of love. Now please understand that sin is bad. It will (as my current Pastor says) take you further than you want to go and keep you longer than you want to stay.

<u>Sin will put the brakes on the plan of God in your life, not because God ceases to love you or ceases to chase you down, but because you step away from loving Him and stop chasing Him.</u> But I'm here to tell you that God is always willing and able to restore you back to a right relationship. <u>He is NOT mad at you</u>. He loves you unconditionally. There's nothing you can do to separate yourself from His love.

After Mitzi and I left the ministry that second time, we moved into a house on the other side of town and to this day, we have no idea how we were able to move in. We had no job, and the only money we had at the time I believe was some leftover tax refund that was going to dry up real fast once the deposit and first month was paid. However, the man who owned the place let us in and we were so excited once again because we were starting over.

The place we moved into was an older house on the corner of a street in Richmond, Indiana. Next door lived a drug dealer and that might be why the place came so cheap and the neighborhood was less than charming, but we didn't care. We had a home and better yet, we didn't have to go back to another homeless shelter.

I had made a close friend, Maurice, while at the school – he was a Pastor of sorts in Richmond but also worked in the kitchen in the Bible College and he was a big help to us during this time. He was a constant encouragement to us and we went to his church and he even let me preach and we got to know each other pretty well.

I tried to find a job while living here, but jobs were pretty scarce and honestly, I just wanted to be back in the ministry but also felt that I had sort of blown my chances of that happening again, so I was stoked to be a vital part of Maurice's life and ministry.

He had such huge dreams and a huge heart. His church was super small – only a couple of people attended and he also lived in a pretty bad part of town, but whenever he could he was helping people – either giving them rides or just talking with them and he wanted to start a soup kitchen there in Richmond to help feed the hungry and he wanted it also to serve as a church as well. It was going to be called "Love's Ministry".

Maurice and I spent a lot of time together talking about the future, about God, about our dreams, and things were looking up for the most part, except I still didn't have a job and my relationship with Mitzi was hit or miss at times. We used to fight a lot in the first years of our marriage.

I still struggled off and on with pornography and this put a huge strain on our relationship. Each time, I would come to Mitzi and apologize and beg her forgiveness and each time she would forgive me and our union would be made strong again and we would seek after God and try to live good, holy, pleasing lives and then back to pornography I would go – it began to be my crutch, my scapegoat.

There were a couple times even when I tried to go back to smoking or drinking but it always made me sick and I didn't want anything to do with that. But with porn, it was different. <u>Here I could still live a public spiritual life and then just do the porn thing on the side when no one was looking.</u> If I got caught, I could just ask for mercy and forgiveness and Mitzi was such a trooper and even though I hurt her so many times, each time she would forgive me.

It's not as though I wasn't sorry, I just wasn't sorry enough to stop. Plus, I still struggled so bad with my identity and I didn't understand at the time that <u>because I saw myself as a loser on the inside, it was stopping me from being a winner on the outside</u> and so the vicious cycle of sin to forgiveness, sin to forgiveness trudged forward and eventually it did become too much for Mitzi.

A few months after moving into the house there in Richmond, Mitzi gave birth to *Isaiah Joshua Zeitz* on November 23rd and this time it was a planned C-section so the hospital visit was more expedited. Also gone were the comforts of the first-time hospital stay where we lounged, ate, and watched television. This time was much quicker and before we knew it, we were back at the house in Richmond, with two babies and no money coming in.

Isaiah Joshua Zeitz

Eventually we racked up 6 months-worth of back rent and yet the landlord didn't kick us out! It was crazy. We deserved to be kicked out and I certainly wasn't doing my best to pay him. I did get one job as a machine operator for $8.00 an hour and that job lasted only a month.

I remember having to dip out molten metal with a giant spoon-like ladle and pour it into a press. Then I would push a button and the machine would slam shut in order to make some part and if you overfilled the metal goo or didn't do everything just right there would be excess molten metal shot into the air that would then come raining down on your neck and it burnt so bad. I went to use the restroom one day and simply slipped out the door, never to return.

Life got really hard before it finally got better. My sin was causing Mitzi to doubt my love for her and she was finally fed up with it all. She called her mother in Wisconsin and told her of her troubles. I remember being so angry that she would go behind my back and call her mom and basically tell on me that I grabbed the phone from her and in a fit of rage, I screamed at her mom to take her in, and away from me.

Mitzi was so hurt and to this day, I regret that decision so much. I left the house that night and stayed in some cheap hotel across town. The next morning, Mitzi's mom arranged for a taxi to pick her and Moriah and Isaiah up from the house and take them to the airport. By the time I got home later that day, they were gone.

The house felt so empty. I cried and cried and cried. I hated so much the man I was becoming. Sin was eating away at my life and robbing me from God's blessings. It was stealing my family, my life, my soul, and I was allowing it to.

The reality of it all hit me hard! I remember during this time, I went to a porn shop of all things across town and I was so scared to go in and I was so ashamed but I did it anyways and upon entering, before even looking around, I had knots all in my stomach and then I spotted a young man whom I had known from Bible college in the shop too!

I could scarcely believe my eyes! Here was this young man, who was also a counselor and a fellow Bible school student in the same porn shop at this very moment! I just remember looking at him and saying, "What are you doing in here?" and of course we both darted out of there as fast as we could – both super ashamed and embarrassed. I did the only thing I knew to do and say, I said, "Hey you want to come, check out my house?"

He reluctantly agreed, probably just happy to be doing anything other than what he was just doing, and we went inside and it was really strange and awkward and I didn't even tell him that Mitzi had left or anything and then he left and went home and that was that.

I'm sure that was not what either of us had planned for that evening, but I'm also sure glad that I saw him in there now, looking back, because it opened my eyes to who I was becoming. Never one time while living at the

Bible school did I know that this man dealt with this addiction, nor he I.

I needed to truly repent and get my family back! I needed to get back what the devil had stolen from me – what I had allowed him to steal! I needed to restore my relationship with God, with Mitzi. <u>I needed to begin to realize that God had greater plans for my life than for me to simply trudge through life, living willy-nilly and not knowing who I was in Him.</u>

That night, I called my mom and asked her for fuel money. She didn't want to give me anything because she thought it good that I learned a tough lesson. In hindsight, I can see that her intentions were pure. Discouraged for the moment but not thwarted, I drove to the Bible College to talk with Miss Martha, the same lady that played the piano during mine and Mitzi's wedding, and I told her the situation. Well, I sort of told her the situation. I told her I needed to get to my dad's house to try and get a job and then I would go and get my family back.

She gave me enough money to get to his house – an hour or so away. That very night, I drove to my dad's and when I got there, surprisingly he was excited to see me and I told him of the situation. He told me that this was not the end of the world and that I would get through this and then he gave me some money and told me to go get a job and help support myself and Mitzi. Although I know to this day, that he knew what I was going to do and he gave me enough to do it! I left that night from Indiana and drove straight through to Wisconsin.

By the time I got there it was the next day and Mitzi was not at her mom's house. She was out with her childhood friend at the doctor's office in an appointment concerning Isaiah. I waited for her to return, and when she did, I told her I was there to take her home. She was not happy at all. In fact, she didn't really want to come with me, but did anyway and the entire trip home was pretty silent.

Mitzi had always known she wanted to be a mom and a wife. She had always known that she wanted to marry a strong man and have adorable children. This was her dream and desire, and she saw this in me when we met! She never asked much of me, just that I would do what I was supposed to do – be a good dad, a loving husband, a spiritual leader. I had failed in all three of these and yet she still loved me. <u>She has always been so faithful to me and stuck by my side in the most trying times!</u>

I found out later that she had taken one of my shirts with her and sprayed it to smell like me to keep with her. I am so thankful to God for His redeeming power. Again, it's not He that does these bad things to us, but it is He who in spite of these bad things can and does use them to bless us and to make us better and stronger.

<u>After Mitzi and I realized that we needed to have God back at the center of our marriage, and after I cried out to Him with my whole heart, we were reconciled not only with each other, but also with Him. God is good all the time and He is a restoration God.</u>

After so much time of us not being able to pay the rent there at the house in Richmond, the landlord was finally forced to kick us out. However, after we left – a few months later we were able to send him a check in the mail to cover the back rent we owed. We used an entire tax check to do so and it was hard watching all that money disappear at once, but we were so glad to do it.

You know sometimes we make decisions that aren't always the best. We rush out and act first only to pay dearly later.

Like the time I bought Mitzi a new camera for Christmas one year and told her and the children, Moriah and Isaiah at the time, not to ever touch the lens because it would ruin the camera. To my utter dismay, the very next day after giving this admonition, (a euphemism for a command) I was mortified to find out that someone had in fact smudged the lens!

I went to take a nice family picture and I wasn't able to do so because of the smudge and no matter how hard I tried the pictures turned out foggy. Immediately, I did the only thing a holy spiritual leader can do in this situation, I yelled at the children demanding to know who touched the lens.

After walking into the next room to cool off for a bit, I came back moments later head hanging low and with a half-smile and a look that begged everyone's mercy, I asked everyone to forgive me and assured them that it was I who was the big jerk here.

You see, I had simply forgotten to put my contacts in that morning!!!

Sometimes we do stupid things. We say stupid things. Sometimes, these stupid things can have some hefty ramifications. However, never confuse consequences with God's best for your life. In other words, God's best for us can sometimes be thwarted, but it's not because that was God's original plan, it's just that we missed it somewhere along the way. But thanks be to Him who is able to do exceeding abundantly above all that we ask or think according to the power that works in us (Ephesians 3:20). Even if we do do (pun here fully intended) a stupid thing, He is able to fix it and restore life and hope and joy in our lives! He is able, if we let Him, to truly give us a fresh start!

14 "HEALING IN HIS WINGS"

"For His anger endureth but a moment; in his favour is life: weeping may endure for a night, but joy cometh in the morning." ~Psalm 30:5 KJV

I called my grandma and told her of our housing situation and she agreed to allow us to live with her until I could find work and so we lived with her and my mom for several months until I finally landed a job at a sub shop in Greenfield, Indiana.

Before this however, Mitzi and I had tried again to move back to Bible College, but the head Pastor wisely told us no. You see, going back there was starting to become a way of escape for us – a way to not have to face reality, but he didn't want us back until we could prove that we were stable enough and so that was our thinking going forward. I was going to make something of myself and then present ourselves before them again sometime in the future.

After landing the job at the sub place, I did pretty well and they promoted me to shift manager and this entailed a small raise and one free sub every day, so for me I was happy enough.

Also during this time, Mitzi and I started walking closer with God and we even had some awesome family times with my cousins and other family members – people that we had never really bonded with before then.

I came up with what was called "The Billy Show," and this was pretty much just an excuse to dress up in

Joshua in "The Billy Show"

weird attire and act as crazy as possible while Mitzi filmed us all. We danced and sang and did all sorts of wild shenanigans.

I also used to walk every morning and many evenings and it was during these times that I drew even closer to

God. I would talk with Him just as I would talk with you. I really learned how to develop an intimacy with Him like I had never had before. Even when I was in jail, I used to quote scriptures and walk but never did I have that one-on-one time with Him like now.

The Bible says that God will never leave us nor forsake us and there were times when I would walk and talk with Him that it felt like He was right there, and can I tell you something amazing?! He was. He is, and He always has been. Ever since giving my life to Christ back in that jail cell, God was trying to have that sort of intimacy with me. He desires so much to commune with us, to move through us to bless and help others, and it was during this time, that I began to do things for others in a way I had never done before.

It wasn't really a chore anymore to give or to serve Him; it was beginning to become a joy to do so. Slowly, the closer I got to God the more I became like Him and it was a great experience.

Mitzi and I moved out of my grandmother's and into a small townhome across town, back in the town I grew up in and it was really nice there – we were right next to the park, within walking distance, and it was here that I spent much of my time with the Lord.

We developed a close relationship with the landlady there as well. Her husband was battling Parkinson's disease and they were both retired. The set of townhomes was the only way she made her income and I began to help out when I could either raking leaves, planting flowers, shoveling snow, cleaning her house, fixing odds and ends and so forth and oftentimes she would make us cookies or make us little crafts and all-in-all it was a good time.

After about a year or so of living there and paying rent and learning to be stable, I decided to move on from working at the sub shop. I wanted to make a little more money and also to try and "make something of myself."

I had dreams of going back to school, but wasn't really sure how to do that. I saw a job posting one day for a corrections officer in a neighboring town and so I decided to apply. It was a state job and given my criminal record, I didn't really think I stood a chance but I filled out the application online anyhow.

To my surprise they called me in for an interview! I went and then they called me back for a second interview. They knew about the felonies on my record because they did a thorough background check – after all this was a state job at a juvenile prison so they had to – and yet they still wanted me to work there.

Mitzi and I were nervous, but we were also excited because this meant new opportunities for us. She had always wanted to live in a nice house with a nice yard and now with the money I was going to be making this could be possible.

Before, whenever I had tried to get a decent job, people would always find out about my record and turn me away. One job in particular -the head hiring guy, told me straight out that had I lied to him about my record, he would have hired me, but now knowing my past, he was obligated not to do so.

This was some of the reason that I had struggled with my self-worth because I always felt like I was stuck working dead-end jobs for minimum wage and that my record was going to keep me from going anywhere in the workplace. I started to allow some of this to rub off on me as a person and then it led me down dark and depressing avenues.

Thanks be to God however, because in His eyes I am the righteousness of God in Christ! And here I was about to go work for the state of Indiana with a professional title, real insurance, benefits, and with a retirement package?! I didn't know anything of the sort.

Up until just a short time prior to this I was still in the process of serving an 11-year probation term and that was miraculously taken care of! God had put it on my heart to go and repaint my dad's garage floor. So, I spent hours moving everything out and cleaning and scrubbing it and then I applied that epoxy paint – the one that has all the mosaic sparkles and stuff in it – and made it look real nice.

He came out to the garage later that day and was moved to tears by what he saw. He had just sold some property and had made a decent amount of money on it and he came out to the garage and handed Mitzi and I a check for $2,500! This was more money than we even knew what to do with. It was an awesome miracle. We were able with that money to pay off my probation fees and with still years left to serve, the judge decided to call it even and annulled my sentence and I was off probation!

Up to this point, I wasn't even allowed to leave the state and living in Richmond, Indiana when we did, so close to Ohio this was difficult to do. God is so good!

Anyhow, I got the job at the prison in spite of my felony record and we were ever so thankful.

I had to go through two weeks of training before I was to become an officer of the state. It was a blast. I got to learn all about prison life and what we would be up against. We had written tests and then we practiced various takedown moves that we might have to use on the inmates and trained in how to handle emergency situations. It was crazy to me, that I had once been on the other side of the fence as an inmate myself and to hear how they spoke about inmates, it was eye-opening and sometimes amusing.

Training was in a place like an hour away from the actual juvenile prison so all of us trainees would meet up at the prison there and take a transport bus together. I was in charge of driving.

One day on the way back home, I received a phone call while driving. I answered and it was the brother of my best friend, Maurice, from Richmond. He said, "I'm sorry to tell you man, but Maurice passed away." He had always struggled with weight issues and sleep apnea and apparently, he laid down to take a nap and forgot to put on his breathing mask and passed away in his sleep.

I was devastated and I thanked him for calling and I drove home in silence, frozen with sadness. I tried my best to push it all away – to save face for those around me. I drove home and pulled Mitzi into the back room and told her. We both just started crying so hard. It hurt so badly and even now writing this out, I'm weeping. It was such a sad time in my life.

I had never had a friend like Maurice before. We shared so many hours together just talking – about God, about life, about dreams for the future, about Love's Ministry. He was 30 years old, had a wife and four children, with one on the way. I loved Maurice. He was the funniest, most happy-go-lucky man I have ever known. <u>He was a constant encouragement to me and I can't wait to see him in heaven!</u>

For a few years after, I struggled with depression, with sadness, and every once in a while, I would get the urge to end my life early even. Sometimes, I would just start crying non-stop if something triggered a memory of Maurice in me like being out to eat at CiCi's Pizza from time to time - even to this day, I will think about him, because we used to go there and eat and just to make everybody laugh, I would stuff brownies all up in my teeth and smile a big chocolate smile to everybody passing by our table. He got such a kick out of that.

Maurice was the best man in my wedding. He was a true man of God and his heart for people was extraordinary. Mitzi bonded with him pretty close as well because He used to sing a lot and she was on the praise team and they would sing together. Needless to say, this whole thing hit us really hard.

The Bible says that weeping may endure for a night, but joy comes in the morning! Sometimes that night can last a long time. For me it lasted a good two years or so, but <u>I'm happy to report that God is a restoration God and He will comfort us in our time of need.</u>

Like I mentioned earlier, He is not a cancer-causing car wrecking creator, He is a loving life-giving Lord, and it wasn't He who took Maurice on to be with Him early to teach us anything, but in spite of Maurice going on to be with the Lord, I have a hope – one day I will see him again and until that happens, I have been redeemed from anger or animosity or depression. God has given me joy in place of sadness, and if we will just allow Him to – He will turn around an unseemly situation or event and make it all better!

I worked at the juvenile there for about a year. It was a crazy time, but I'm so thankful for the experience. I even got to become a certified member of the quick response team and during training they spray you with OC – which is like a grade above normal pepper spray. Anyhow, I was dumb enough to say, "I can't even feel it," after which the instructor sprayed me again, this time directly in my eyes and whew!! I felt it then.

I always thought it was neat how I spent about the same amount of time as a Corrections Officer as I did as an inmate. It's crazy how God can bring us full circle and completely redeem our past.

After leaving the juvenile, Mitzi and I had to move out of our new house we were able to rent with the money I was making. It was hard at first to move, but in hindsight, I'm glad I don't work there anymore. The people that do that job are to be applauded because it can be quite taxing on you physically and emotionally, especially working with the teenage population.

We bounced around a bit more after that before finding ourselves in need once again of a home. After having come back from making so much money at the juvenile, it was difficult for me to process getting a job again as a cook making minimum wage and so after working at Olive Garden for a short season (no pun intended); I quit and decided that I wanted something more with my life. I still had yet to learn that if you don't work you don't eat wisdom principle from the Bible and I felt that God would provide no matter what I did.

I was wrong and we ended up without a home once again! Some friends from church were gracious enough to take us in and while living at their house, I got more involved in the local church. The church offered me a job as their janitor. It wasn't a ton of money, but I was thankful for it and Mitzi was too.

During this time, I started going out to my uncle's farm to help him with the milking and various chores. I didn't get paid for much, but I was happy to help. All along I was learning the value of hard work and I was able to be a blessing to him. Given the fact that he had to milk the cows every day, he was never able to leave for extended periods of time or go on vacation. After I learned the ropes a bit there, he was able to trust me to milk the cows and bottle the milk and so he could finally get away.

It was a neat experience working there and again I am so thankful for having had that time. Keep in mind; this is the same uncle I used to steal money from in order to service my drug addiction years earlier so again this was another full-circle redemption moment from God!

After moving out of the nice couple's home from church, one of the elders of the church came to Mitzi and me one day and told us he had been trying to rent out a house of his to no avail and would be happy to have us live there free of charge or at least until he could sell it. We were ever so happy to oblige his proposition!

We lived at his house for quite a while and it was during this time that we had the job at the church cleaning and also working on the farm. It was a really neat experience living here as well because we had a lot of family time! We were within walking distance of the movie store that gave free kids movies and we were also close to the pizza shop so we had many pizza and movie nights.

Now before I end this chapter, we must rewind because you are not aware of the fact that we had three children by now! You see back when I was working in the juvenile Mitzi and I had been trying to have another child for quite some time to no avail.

We finally did get pregnant and were so excited! However, a short month or so later, Mitzi miscarried and it was another tough time in our life. We were not near as thrown back by this as we were with Maurice passing away, because we had learned by now to praise God in spite of our circumstances. So, we kept trying for another baby.

I always wanted to have lots of children – like 12 or more! However, we were happy to try and at least have one more. One day Mitzi wrapped a present for me to open - I opened it and inside was a positive pregnancy test. She was beaming with joy as was I!

After leaving the job with the juvenile, we moved back into the townhomes we once stayed for a short spell when I worked at Olive Garden. It was then that Mitzi gave birth to *Josiah Samuel Zeitz* on April 15th.

There were some complications after his birth because he was a bit premature and still had fluid in his lungs. Mitzi didn't even get to hold him afterwards because they put him under a breathing tent and transported him immediately to a children's hospital. He stayed there for a little while and Praise God he was completely well and came out all the better!

Josiah Samuel Zeitz

I have been saying it all along and I will say it again, God is good! He can make something out of nothing and He can turn our sorrow into dancing, our sadness into joy, He can take us from being a Victim to a Victor if we let Him.

In this chapter I have shared with you some pretty tough times in my life and in the life of my family, we moved around some more, we were homeless a few more times (although never fully, praise the Lord!), we experienced the changing of jobs, the changing of lifestyle, we went through much grief and loss, and

yet we experienced new life through the birth of Josiah and I got to draw closer to God in a way like never before! I learned more how to hear His voice and was constantly reminded of how much He loves me.

I did some stupid things sure, like quitting a job before finding another one and yet God had mercy on me. The Bible says His mercies are new every morning. If we are waiting to be perfect before asking for God's help, we are going to be waiting a very long time and if we think that God only helps those who help themselves then we are missing the fact that Christ died for us while we were lost in sin and could do nothing of the sort. If we are waiting to be accepted by other people before we are willing to step out and accept others, we are missing the point of what it truly means to be Christ-like.

If you notice, I didn't mention anything about pornography or sin in this chapter and rightly so. Was I tempted? Yes. Did I sin at all during this whole time? Yes. But was I oh so consumed with it all? No. And this is what God was trying to teach me the whole time – not by causing bad things to happen, but instead in spite of these things happening. I was able to work for my uncle and be happy even though I wasn't getting paid because I wasn't all consumed with myself. I was learning to be a giver.

During this time, I had the opportunity to go back to the Bible College Mitzi and I had left, except this time they invited me as a guest speaker! Can you believe it? Mitzi sang a beautiful song and I preached for far too long, but it was an awesome experience and I got to share a little bit of my life to the teenagers there and for me all the hurt and the pain that I had gone through after Maurice died, it all seemed to melt away!

Pastor Jim is always saying that we need to have purpose beyond our pain and when we do; we will find that God heals us in the process.

God is good and if we will just trust in Him we will find healing in his wings...

"My Friend"

"Looking unto Jesus the author and finisher of our faith; who for the joy that was set before him endured the cross, despising the shame, and is set down at the right hand of the throne of God." ~Hebrews 12:2 (KJV)

"A man that hath friends must shew himself friendly: and there is a friend that sticketh closer than a brother." ~Proverbs 18:24 (KJV)

"Wherefore seeing we also are compassed about with so great a cloud of witnesses, let us lay aside every weight, and the sin which doth so easily beset us, and let us run with patience the race that is set before us ." ~Hebrews 12:1 (KJV)

You were my friend.
You were my friend.
You were my friend,
and I'll see you again.
I said I'll see you again.
You were my friend.
You were my friend.
You were my friend,
can't wait to see you again.
I can't wait to see you again,
to see you again.

Sittin' on the front porch rockin'!
Times tickin' by, but who's clockin' it!
I don't even care cause I'm mockin' it!
So mad that that you're gone,
Put a sock in it!!
I keep lying to myself,

Like I'm over it.
I miss you so much,
I can't cope with it.
Your brother told me that you passed,
and I rolled with it.
On the job workin', so I flowed with it.
I got home, told my wife,
but the words,
man I choked on 'em.
Lookin' for escape,
Where's the opening?
Looking for His grace,
Where's the hope in it?
God help me please,
cause I'm fumbling!

They tell me time heals all,
yet I'm strugglin'.
Fightin' back the tears,
I remember when;
you and me, we used to preach so hard,
we were lovin' it.
Love's ministry,
that's what we called it.
Plans for the future,
but you squashed it!
The day you fell asleep forever,
you drew your last breath,
and I didn't have a clue,
rest in peace Maurice.

I wish I knew!
I wish I knew!!
I wish I knew!!!

You were my friend.
You were my friend.
You were my friend,
and I'll see you again.
I said I'll see you again.
You were my friend.
You were my friend.
You were my friend,
can't wait to see you again.
I can't wait to see you again,
to see you again.

Chillin' in the Laundromat,
Eatin' up the M&M's;
not the rapper.
I'd toss the wrapper,
for one more day with you.
Just to tell you how I feel,
what I've been going through.
Two Izaiah's, but not spelled the same.
I got another boy, but he don't know your name.
Look, I know you're in a better place.
It ain't the same!
It's still lame!
Without you here,
sometimes I start crying.
Without you near,
Lord knows I've been trying.
I was angry for the longest time.
Those long nights of prayer,
"Word of God Speak,"
it was blastin'.
You knelt down at the altar,

while I prayed in the back.
The God Team baby,
man, I wish it was back!
Runnin', runnin',
trying to make a hundred.
Sleepin' at the movies,
long talks in the car.
Best man at my wedding,
man, we came so far!
Brownies in my teeth,
we was having a ball.
Cookouts at the house,
brown sugar and all.
I miss you my friend,
Enjoy your reward Maurice.
I'll see you again!

You were my friend.
You were my friend.
You were my friend,
and I'll see you again.
I said I'll see you again.
You were my friend.
You were my friend.
You were my friend,
can't wait to see you again.
I can't wait to see you again,
to see you again.

Lord, it wouldn't be the same,
lest I ended with you.
My friend passed away,
but you helped pull me through.
You endured the cross,

for the joy set before you.
Surely I can bear this minimal separation.
Eternity is waiting, I'll be patient.
"Word of God Speak."
God reigns!
Are you hurting, tired, lost, or afraid?
He'll take the pain, break the chains,
make depression move away.
I know it hurts, I know it aches.
Invite him in!
That's all it takes!
The same God that numbers our hair,
He knows our pain!
He took our place!
He hears your cries!
He knows your name!
Lord, it wouldn't be the same,
lest I ended with you.
My friend passed away,
but your helping me through.

You are my friend.
You are my friend.
You are my friend,
and I'm letting you in.
I said I'm letting you in.
You are my friend.
You are my friend
You are my friend,
and I'm letting you in.
I said I'm letting you in!

I love you Lord!!! (My Best Friend!!!)
     By: Joshua Zeitz

Write it out!

It took me quite some time to fully "get over" the fact that Maurice passed away and there are times even to this day that I will cry, wishing he was here. However, I am not mad at God, nor am I without hope, because I know that Maurice had a relationship with Jesus and is living with Him forever!

Perhaps you have lost someone you care about. Perhaps there are things that you have been holding onto for quite some time – be it anger, lust, pride, jealousy, hurt, shame, whatever it is, I wanted to give some space here just for you – so that you could express these struggles and feelings on the lines provided and then I want to pray for you afterwards.

I want you to know that God is not mad at you and it is not He who causes bad things to happen in our life. He loves you. Take some time to write whatever it is you want to write on the lines provided and then with your whole heart, cry out to God, agree with me in prayer that God will comfort you in this time and help you get through whatever it is that has been weighing on you:

_____

_____

_____

_____

_____

_____

_____

_____

_____

_____

_____

"Casting all your care upon him; for he careth for you."
~1Peter 5:7 (KJV)

"Father, In Jesus' Name, I come boldly before you, not based on what I have done or haven't done, but based on what Jesus has done for me and I ask that you help me in this time of need. I cast all my care upon you, according to your Word, believing that you care for me. In Jesus' name, Amen."

Whatever it is that you wrote down, please know that God loves you in spite of it all. That He wants to heal you, to deliver you, to give you hope and peace.

Perhaps you don't have the confidence to believe that prayer above because you haven't yet begun a relationship with Jesus or maybe you have been far from him. Please know that you can have a relationship with Him right now, just repeat this simple prayer and believe it with your whole heart:

"Jesus, I believe that you died just for me. I believe that you were raised from the dead just for me. I believe that you shed your blood so that I could be forgiven and be restored to God. Jesus, come into my heart. Come into my life. Forgive me, cleanse me, and make me a new creation. Satan and Sin, I turn my back on you. Jesus, I turn to you now. Thank you for coming into my heart Jesus and today, right now I begin a new relationship with you. In your name I pray Jesus, Amen."

If you would like further information on accepting Jesus as your Savior and living a Joy filled life, feel free to contact me at:: captivatedhope@gmail.com

15 "JOYFULLY EVER AFTER"

Up until now, I have desired to share with you some of the struggles and things I have gone through since being born-again and I hope that you can see that even the darkest times that I have shared thus far in part two are not to be compared at all to those within part one and the main reason that I hope stands out for this is: Jesus!

You see even in our darkest times as a Christian, we have hope. We can know even in the midst of extreme loss that there is more to life than this and that this place, the place we call home – Earth even – is not really our home, but instead my home is in Heaven with Him – the one who saved me, who redeemed my life from sin, from death, from destruction!

I have come to learn that Jesus is the reason for the season – the season of life – and that when I take my last breath here on this Earth, all that truly matters is not what I have gotten, but rather what I have given away, and we can't give what we don't have. Therefore, it is important that we learn to trust in God and live our life in Him so that He can then move through us to bless the lives of others.

The Bible says the first will be last and those who would seek to be the greatest must be servant of all. I have had to learn this lesson the hard way many times and it's not that God wanted me to learn it the hard way, but rather that I was either stubborn or was simply never taught a better way and God's way is always better.

After Mitzi and I and the children left the house we were living in for free, (we had to leave because the man was finally ready to rent it out), we were homeless once more and so the church agreed that we could live in their garage! We stayed there for a night or two before I think they realized that having three small children sleeping on old dusty pews was not going to do and allowed us to sleep inside.

Mitzi and I were talking about this the other day and she said she was so thankful that the children were young during this time because they don't remember much and while it is true, I also know that even if we were living under a bridge tonight, they wouldn't complain. We have been blessed with such awesome children.

Those few weeks we stayed there in the church were a blast! The children and I used to crawl all over the floor in the sanctuary playing tag and wrestling and all the while Mitzi and I just believed for God to provide.

Things were different now than before. I had been learning the value of hard work. I was beginning to understand that God and family go before ministry. In the past, I had always done things opposite – I did ministry work in order to try and get God to do things for me – almost like I was trying to buy His love. Now however, I was slowly learning that it was more important to see myself as God saw me – to BE the man of God He called me to be – to love Him with all my heart, mind, and strength and to love Mitzi as Christ loved the church and gave Himself for it.

The closer Mitzi and I got to God, the more He

began to show us new and exciting things. He began to show us creative ways to give – to bless others. He was showing me that ministry was work and that work was good as long as we did it in His strength not our own.

We held a breakfast event where we invited people from the community to come and eat. I fixed breakfast for everyone. Mitzi had started a women's choir where they sang and did special things for the holidays. I even tried to learn how to play the drums so I could help out the praise leader. I did a decent 4-4 beat but that's all I could muster!

I was given the opportunity to preach on Mother's Day and at other times and it was really neat to be able to preach to much more "seasoned" youth than myself and to hear some of their reactions afterward!

Our time at the church and really the whole time we were moving from here to there after the juvenile was a blessed time. We never had much money, but we gave what we had away. We never had a solid job, but we worked for others.

We had come to prove that although we may not have been the wisest financially we did have what it took to be in the ministry and one day after receiving a phone call from our old Pastor at the Bible College, he invited us to come back and work there again.

This time however, we were older and wiser (granted, these two things don't always go together) and much more hesitant than to simply jump ship from what we were doing and go there even if it did mean a job and a house - and it did mean those things. They offered us a nice home and a nice job and the children would be going to school there and it was going to all work out.

We drove all the way to Richmond and met with the Pastor. The leadership was impressed with us and yet while in the meeting, something just felt off. You see by this time, I had learned more how to hear the voice of

God and something was telling me no.

A few days later, the Pastor called to tell us that they had changed their minds about the house we would be living in and it would be a much smaller place instead. Mitzi knew right away that it was a no, but I was still a bit hesitant thinking again that the children wouldn't mind and they would have a nice school and all but again it just didn't feel right and we both agreed.

I called the Pastor back and told him that we just didn't feel like it was the right move and we respectfully denied his offer. He was taken back a bit and I believe to this day that had we taken that position, it would have been the wrong move. A few years later, the Bible College and the entire ministry there shut down and I'm so thankful that God spared us from all of that!

I began to pray more about what God wanted from us and I kept feeling as though we needed to leave Indiana and start over. A year prior, my grandmother had moved to Tennessee to live close to my aunt and uncle who had moved a couple years prior (the same Aunt Beth Fox who wrote the foreword for this book).

I called my grandma and told her what I was feeling and hearing and she agreed to let us come down there and live with her again until we could find a job. We packed up all our belongings into a rented U-Haul truck and hitched it to the back of our minivan and drove down to Tennessee.

It was a crazy drive too because I had been born and raised in Indiana all my life – the roads there are flat as can be and once we hit Kentucky and into Tennessee, I was literally gripping the steering wheel so tight – I thought for sure we were going to fall off the edge of the Earth!

We stayed with my grandma for about a year until I got a job as a breakfast cook and a dessert maker at a university in Nashville. I worked there for a little over a year before Mitzi started a daycare business out of our little townhouse. We have been doing daycare now for about seven years in Tennessee.

Shortly after coming to Tennessee, Mitzi started looking for churches around the area that were non-denominational and she found one called Joy Church International in Mt. Juliet, Tennessee (visit: https://joychurch.net/). Now I hadn't really wanted anything to do with church since leaving Indiana because we had poured so much into the last one with very little to show for it.

Mitzi and I were doing so many cool things there at the church and giving to people – we held lock-ins for the teens and children, we were trying to get the church to grow and move forward, but every time we would take a step forward, it seemed like we were met with stringent opposition and then would go two steps back. It wasn't until years later that I finally learned under Pastor Jim, that you can't change a church or a business for that matter from the bottom-up; it has to come from the top-down.

The Pastor there was getting up in age and I expected him to teach me the ropes and perhaps pass on the reigns to me but it just never worked out and again I am certain that wouldn't have been the right move anyhow.

Regardless, I was still dealing with some rejection and hurt that can come with misguided ministry and I was extremely cautious about getting back into another situation like that.

Mitzi finally convinced me to go and check it out and so we went. When we pulled up, there were people standing in the parking lot waving at us and then I saw the sign and it said "International" on it. Here we were in little Mt. Juliet at this not-so-giant church and it says International? I thought this has to be some kind of nut house. I did NOT want to go in but Mitzi finally convinced me to at least try it and so I did.

We went inside and the entire praise team was color-coordinated and everybody was all smiling and happy and I thought to myself, this has to be some kind of cult! I joked with Mitzi "When are they going to pass the Kool-Aid?!"

A man got up and asked everyone to raise their hands if they were new and of course I did not! Pastor Jim however still found his way over to us and shook our hands. He seemed very genuine and as soon as he began to preach, I just knew that this was a man of God and we were hooked.

Since being in Tennessee and at Joy Church, Mitzi and I have gotten better in our marriage, our finances, our child rearing, and especially our personal walks with God. We have been much more stable in our home life – we lived at our first place for four years, and the place we are in now, going on three!

I know looking back at some of these things we have gone through, some of you might be thinking, "Wow, what's wrong with you Josh!" and rightly so. I mean I was the cause of many of the heartbreaks we went through simply because I wasn't living in wisdom.

I don't want to make any excuses or play the victim ever. I believe that God does give wisdom through His word and He will empower us to do things, but I also want you to understand that Mitzi and I – when we first met, we knew very little about life. Just the other day, Mitzi and I were watching some show and I looked at her and said, "You know we used to be so dumb!" She laughed, and said something to the effect that we still are (learning so many things that is).

Her mom had always done everything for her and even up into the first couple years of our marriage, her mom paid our cell phone bill. Mitzi didn't know how to cook, she didn't drive. She never had any money – ever.

When we worked at the Bible College, we made $50 a week and so it was simply used to spend on food and entertainment.

Me, I learned how to drive when I was 12 or 13 because my dad used to let us take the wheel out on the country roads. He taught us how to cook, to clean, I had a job when I was 14 and kept it until I was 17 and I knew how to put money away.

So, I knew much more than she did in many aspects, but in matters like keeping a job, loving a wife, raising a child, duty, honor, respect, giving, and so forth I was so ignorant. We never had anyone to come alongside us and tell us how to have a good, successful marriage, how to balance a checkbook, how to pay bills, (I remember one time, I had to call my mom and ask her how to send a letter in the mail because I didn't know where my name and address should go compared to the recipient), how to live godly, how to be a man - a leader.

I wanted so bad to have someone I could look up to, someone I could learn under, but all the people we knew were always telling us what we needed to do, never how to do it. And Mitzi – she would always get the brunt of it especially from family, because they never wanted to confront me on certain issues – perhaps they were intimidated, I don't know. For whatever reason, people would all the time tell Mitzi, "You know Josh needs to get a job." "Josh needs to smile more." "What's wrong with Josh? Is he mad?"

She would always defend me and she tried as best as she could to be the best wife and mother, and yet she too lacked any real role model in her life to follow after.

Now, again I don't want you to hear excuses or think that I am pitching a sob story, I am simply telling it how it was and because of all this, that's why I am so thankful to now be in a church that not only tells us what to do, but they teach us how to do it.

Pastor Jim and his wife live out their successful marriage in front of us. The staff and leadership there live and lead by example what it truly means to be in full-time ministry and we have learned so much! I know that when God does call us back into the ministry, we are going to be ready this time because we are learning how to live with integrity, with character. We are learning about money and about raising children and are given wisdom principles straight from the Bible and Pastor Jim nuggets – we love them!!

Eight years we have sat under solid Biblical teaching, save for the year we took off from going to church because we were dealing heavily with some family issues and rejection – and how I wish we wouldn't have done that. But we did, and now God has redeemed that as well and made us more the better for it! ("Please be encouraged! God did not call us to live out of our rear-view mirror, we can't undo the choices we've made, but we can learn from it, laugh at it, and then let it go!" ~Pastor Jim)

God is so good! He has taught us so much through Joy Church and <u>we have experienced so many victories in our life, in our marriage, in our family because we have allowed Him to work in us and have allowed Him to use us to bless others!</u>

One of the main things that we have learned is that serving God and going to church or reading our Bibles, it's a get-to not a have-to and by simply changing our perspective on these things, we have gained a new freedom and joy like never before.

Another main thing we have come to learn is to focus on do-do and not the don't-do. I know it sounds a bit funny to hear and the pun here is fully intentional, but in the past both Mitzi and I were quite legalistic and religious at times in our thinking.

There would be huge spans of time when we

didn't watch any movies and the only television we watched was "Christian." (Not that any of that is wrong, but we were doing it to try and appease God - yet, we must learn to come to God by what Jesus has done for us, on His merit alone!) We spoke what is known as "Christianese" within the church world which basically consists of using all sorts of Biblical-sounding terms like "sanctified" without ever really knowing what these things meant.

In essence, a Pastor told me once – he said, "You don't want to become so spiritual-minded, that you're no earthly good." And at the time, I wasn't trying to hear that because I always saw myself as quite spiritual – I mean after all I was radically saved in jail and so forth and for the longest time I was just plain dumb in the things of God and how to truly live out a holy life.

<u>You see Mitzi and I tried to do outwardly what we hadn't yet received inwardly and this got us into a lot of trouble.</u> All the time, I would say and think "Don't-do." And yet I would keep doing those things I didn't want to do or those things I knew not to do. It wasn't until we started to focus on the "Do-Do" that we actually started to see victory in our lives.

Do read the Bible because you get to, Do give because you get to, Do worship and praise God even when you don't feel like it because you get to…It's so amazing how when we get our eyes off of ourselves and onto God and serving others from a "get to" mentality how we look back one day and say, "Wow, I have come so far!"

For Mitzi and I that is exactly how it has been since coming to Tennessee and into Joy – every time we have stopped giving and focusing on ourselves and our own problems – every time we magnified the problem – the problem got bigger and we were unhappy. <u>Yet, every time we have magnified God and focused on giving and</u>

<u>finding purpose beyond our pain, we have been blessed and we have joy!</u> It's an amazingly simple and Biblical principle and if we will just hear and do it we will be blessed!

The Bible says, "Give and it shall be given unto you…" (Luke 6:38) and this is so true. I have found it to be true in my own walk with God and in my everyday life. Whenever I am feeling down or depression tries to come back and rear its ugly head, and I choose to do the Word instead and give someone an encouraging note, or make cookies for someone else, or give someone a gift or simply do small things for my wife or children, I am happy and so full of joy and wouldn't you know it – whatever it was that I was so worried about, just melts away!

I am finally after all these years learning that in order to gain life, you have to give it and as Pastor Jim is always saying, you have to sow where you want to go. If you want money, sow it. If you want respect, sow it. If you want a friend, be one.

Mitzi and I have been through a lot together and have had many victories and seen many miracles, more than what is contained here, in just these few pages, but the main purpose for me adding this part two to my testimony is to show you that God is good and that you too can have an intimate personal relationship with Him.

Perhaps you have found yourself away from God or maybe there has been hurt or rejection or addiction that has stolen your peace and robbed your life or family. Perhaps you have been the major cause of it? I know I was in many instances, but what I also want you to know is that God is good and He loves you so much that He sent His Only Son into this world to die for you and even if you were the only one, He would have done it.

I have done some stupid things. I have messed up. I

haven't always lived the most holy or perfect life, but through it all I have learned to trust in Jesus. I have learned to be a giver – to be like Him.

He is a healer. He will heal your broken heart, your body, your family, whatever it is that you may be struggling with – He will turn it around, use it for His glory in spite of it all – If you let Him.

Will you let Him? If you do not have a personal relationship with Jesus, if you died right now and are not 100% certain where you would go, either Heaven or Hell, you can know right now by giving your life over to Jesus! He loves you and died for you and now He ever lives for you!

Or perhaps you have been saved, you have been born -again and are just living apart from God's best for your life and you want to be reconciled to Him, you can be, right now! I'm not saying there won't be consequences for your actions, there will be, but God is a redeeming God!! He can turn it all around!

Cry out to Jesus now; accept Him as your Lord and Savior. Repent of your sins – turn your back on them and turn to Jesus instead and ask Him to come into your life and save you, make you a new creature – He will!

Happiness is so temporal. It is based on happenings – on circumstances – and circumstances change like the weather, they are good one day and not so good the next. Joy however is a choice! It's a get-to, not a have-to and you can have Joy in spite of the good or not so good. I pray that God will show you His goodness and that this goodness will draw you into His loving arms. I pray that you will taste and see how Good He Is, I pray you will learn to live JOYFULLY EVER AFTER!

Mitzi and Joshua
at the Gaylord Hotel in Nashville
after winning the Great Date Giveaway
from Joy Church.

16 "THE *IAH'S* HAVE IT"
BONUS CHAPTER

I was out walking this morning and the Lord impressed upon my heart to include this bonus chapter, so here we go…

Sometimes, it can be difficult to articulate what we truly mean or want to fully say through the written word alone and so using things like pictures or other visual representations will help the reader understand more fully what is being said.

In light of this and along this same vein of thinking, Mitzi and I believe that children are a good representation of parents. They can be a picture for others to see what is sometimes difficult to put into words.

Granted now however that this does not apply to every family, nor is this meant to be an exact formula. However, in my own life and in our family, I wanted to give you a closer look at our children so you could better see the scope of God at work in our lives.

159

If you remember, a few chapters back, I told you of how I never thought I was going to live to see the age of 20. In Part I, you get a glimpse of why I thought this way. I lived and breathed evil and I did some really reckless things, especially when I was high or drunk.

Fast-forward a few years after that and here Mitzi and I are - both having grown up in dysfunctional and/or broken homes and so there is no reason why our children should not have grown up the same way we did right? I mean after all it is heavily taught in some circles that we are simply a product of our environment.

Yet, here's the GOOD NEWS! Jesus Christ and a relationship with Him can bring about a new future and a new hope into our lives. In Him, we become new creations and no matter what our past might have looked like or what our future looks like, He can and will cause us to become victorious. The Bible says we are more than conquerors through Him that loved us. (Romans 8:37)

If you were to step into my realm of living, right now, you would see children that reflect something so far removed from some of the things that I have written about in this book that you might be hard-pressed to believe much of it.

To this day, when I tell people of my past life and the things I used to be involved in, they oftentimes tilt their head to the side a little, stare at me for a moment and say something like, "Nah, really? I can't even tell by looking at you!" And they are simply mind-blown by the change that God has done in my life.

Better still, when people see our children – and all praise and glory to God – they oftentimes come to Mitzi and me and say something along these lines – "You have such amazing children! They are so well behaved and their love for God can really be seen, you two are such good parents."

Now not everybody says all these things at once, I am simply bringing together in one statement some of the things we have heard from various people. I cannot tell you enough how much this blesses my heart and it will oftentimes bring tears to my eyes because I understand where I used to be, I understand where Mitzi and I have come from, and to have children that now reflect the change in us rather than our old selves, is another testament to the awesome restoration power of God!!!

Truth be told, our children have been such an amazing blessing to us, to me and they have shown me time and time again how much God cares for me and how much He truly desires to have a relationship with us.

Just last night, at the time of this writing, my daughter – Moriah – sent me a text before she went to sleep, now I was already asleep by this time, but I read it this morning and it blessed my socks off!! I want to share it with you, exactly as she wrote it:

Goodnight daddy I love you sooooooooooo... much you mean the world to me and I love you so much.
My father is:
_____

Faithful
Amazing
Triumphant
Handsome
Exquisite
And Real

_____

And you always have been and always will be my dad ☐ goodnight ☐☐ I love you so much more then I can even tell you see you in the morning.☐☐

Wow! What A Blessing!! It gives me allergies so bad! This is what we have started to say in our household whenever someone is getting emotional – we say, "Oh, I'm not crying, it's just my allergies!"

Moriah is so awesome! She is 13 years of age. She has the most extraordinary heart. She goes out of her way to make friends at church. She is so creative. She is always drawing something or doing some sort of craft. She loves to read. I call her "the girl who couldn't stop reading!" (She takes after her mom in this respect.)

Her heart is on fire for the Lord and she desires to be a blessing to all those around her. Just this last year, she has come out of her shell even more and now she is more involved in church – she helps organize and clean, she helps once a month with the little babies, she is a huge help at home with the daycare, she helps greet new comers at church in youth group, I can't say enough of how proud I am of her.

Many girls her age – during this point in their life – especially with all the physical changes going on are oftentimes moody or mean or distant, but she is quite the opposite. In fact, since becoming a teenager, she has stepped out even more! She has purposed in her heart that she is not going to be like what the world expects teenagers to be, so, she has made it her mission to choose joy even when she doesn't feel like it.

She desires to have a closer walk with God and wants to be able to hear His voice, just like her daddy and this is just amazing to me.

She never ceases to make me and her mom laugh either. She definitely gets her crazy side from me, but she is so beautiful just like her mama!

Isaiah Joshua, our first-born son, is the sweetest child I have ever known. He will go out of his way to give me a hug or just say, "I love you." Being just a little younger than his sister, he has always followed her around quite a bit, but he has never been hidden by her shadow. He is definitely his own person. He loves and I mean LOVES Minecraft! The things that child can do on that game is mind-blowing and it's crazy because he will, on his own, research out different builds or things to do and then he will just do it.

This past year or so he has really come out of his shell as well. Every week, I'm there to greet him when he comes out of children's church and he always tells me what they learned and how the class behaved.

Ever since he was really little, Isaiah has always been the sweetest boy. He is really smart. He is quiet, but he is a thinker – like me. He definitely likes to process things before jumping right in or simply speaking his mind and he also has a touch of crazy as well – especially when he is excited about something.

He never ceases to amaze me how smart and funny he is. I think oftentimes, because he didn't communicate like the other two, we thought him to be misbehaving or rebellious. But we finally started to realize, by raising more than one child and also by having a daycare for so many years, that not all children are the same. What works for one child, may not work for the next.

Moriah's attitude has always been, "Just discipline me and get it over with so I can move on." Isaiah on the other hand, has always needed a gentler touch (not that he didn't get disciplined), but he just needed that little bit of extra attention. Through practice, grace, and wisdom Mitzi and I (me especially) have learned how to deal with him in a manner that is best suited to him.

Isaiah is growing up to be an awesome young man in the Lord. He too is a big help around the house and with the daycare. He is definitely more of a mama's boy and I have grown to appreciate that in him.

I have to be careful because he won't let me get away with anything! If I say something to him or his mom or the other children, he holds me to it and I respect this passion and loyalty in him. He has such a kind and sensitive heart and I now have learned that he is much more like me than I cared to admit in the past.

For the longest time, it was always Moriah and Isaiah. They stuck together like glue. It's crazy because whenever they went to children's church they were together. Whenever they went to sleepovers, they were together. Mitzi and I have always encouraged a close relationship between the children because we don't want them to grow up and regret not having one – we want them to stick up for each other, to learn how to love one another.

We were perfectly happy having the two children, but always desired to have more – if you remember I had said I wanted to have 12!

We tried for quite some time but to no avail and then when Mitzi finally did get pregnant again only to miscarry, we began to lose hope a bit, but praise be to God who is faithful and *Josiah Samuel Zeitz* was born on April 15th, 2009.

I remember going in as a family to have that first ultrasound done to check whether the new baby was going to be a boy or girl and Moriah – who was quite little at the time, had wanted a sister really bad. She started crying when we found out it was to be a boy! She got over it quick however and to this day, she and Josiah have a special bond.

Josiah is a boy after my own heart. He is a worshiper. Several people, including the children's Pastor at Joy Church have come to Mitzi or me just to tell us how awesome it was/is to watch Josiah worship the Lord – raising his hands and crying out to God with his whole heart.

He has a heart that is hungry to please God and his love for the scriptures; even at this young age is inspiring! Just the other day, on the way home from church, Josiah was in the backseat quoting all sorts of Bible verses to his brother and sister, telling them which were his favorite.

He, like Isaiah, likes to keep me accountable and he is not afraid to remind me of things I've said – and it's not disrespectfully, they just have that passion to see our family thrive.

He has always been the most outgoing of the three children, always willing to make new friends – no matter where we are or what we are doing, if there are other children around who are close to his age, Josiah will befriend them before we are done doing whatever it is we are doing, even if it's just standing in line for something.

He loves to sing as well. Whenever we are in the car, he is in the backseat just singing his heart out – and he is so dramatic with his singing too, very passionate. When we pray, he likes to be the one to pray as well and he always tries to pray from his heart and he truly believes that he receives what he is asking for!

Josiah has been such an inspiration to me! He truly has a servant's heart. Almost every day, he will come to me and say, "Dad, you need anything? Is there anything I can do to help you?" and I'm learning to get better about finding something for him, because I don't ever want to stop that desire in him to serve.

Every time we go to the grocery store, Mitzi and Moriah usually run inside to grab something and he will unbuckle his seatbelt and come up behind me and start massaging my neck. Isaiah will use this opportunity to talk with me about Minecraft or what other cool thing he learned that day.

Every day, one or all of these children will tell Mitzi and me that they love us. They love to give hugs, to do little things just to bless us. They truly are remarkable children and I give all the glory to God and I am so thankful to Him for them!

I asked Josiah last night, "What do you want to do when you grow up?" he was like, "I don't know…" Rephrasing the question a bit, because I know how daunting that question can be, I said, "Okay, if you could do anything right now, what would you want to do?" He said, "Help people."

What a blessing from the Lord! To have children that are hungry for the things of God – are hungry to be a blessing to others – who are hungry to serve Him with their whole hearts.

I pray these children will continue to grow closer to the Lord, that they will serve Him all the days of their lives, that they will not turn to the left or to the right, but that they would be taught of Him, that they would learn to His voice and want to obey Him, because they know He has the best for them. I pray for their future spouses, that they will be godly, eschewing evil and desire to be givers as well.

I pray that you, as you read this, see more clearly through them that God is a restorer! That He can and will bring newness of life to us! – that you see more clearly through these children, God has blessed Mitzi and me with, that no matter how far one has fallen or however bleak someone's future may look, that God can turn it all around!

Moriah, Isaiah, and Josiah – I love you! I am so proud of you! Thank you for desiring to serve God, for being such awesome children, for teaching me to be a better dad and husband, friend, and ultimately a better man of God – a better Christian.

God gave me a new life and a new heart,
and the *iah's* have it…

Moriah *Isaiah*
Josiah

My 3 "iah's"

Moriah
Isaiah
Josiah

PROLOGUE

What a blessing it has been to revisit some of the past experiences that I have had – some good and some not so good, but nevertheless to revisit them now in light of eternity – after being born-again, and after having developed a personal, intimate relationship with Jesus even the most trying ones are not so bad given the fact that God is so good and that I have been so freed.

On that note, I wanted to encourage you because it can be tempting to read stories such as mine, or others of more prominent figures than me, and remove ourselves from the equation. What I mean is this: We read a powerful story or testimony and we think, "Well that's awesome, God must really love him or her," or "Good for them, but that could never happen to me."

Whatever the case may be, I want to encourage you not to remove yourself from the equation. But rather my prayer is that as you have read some of the thoughts, struggles, or victories I have had, that you have seen yourself in them as well. Granted you may not have battled with the exact things I have, but the Bible is clear that all have sinned and fallen short of the glory of God (Romans 3:23). This should actually give us hope not discouragement. Because if God can change me, if God can answer my prayers, if God loves me, then He most certainly can and will do the same for you.

I previously mentioned that I struggled with pornography for quite some time. It began with a seed sown into my life as a small child and bloomed into a major issue in my teen years, all the way up to the time I was born-again in jail. After being saved, upon allowing the enemy to come in and swallowing his lies, I then struggled with it in the beginning years of my marriage.

Perhaps you are reading this book and there is something that you have been struggling with for quite some time – perhaps it is pornography as well. Whatever addiction you may battle, again I want to encourage you! I am not some special case, God transformed me and freed me and He will do the same for you, if you let Him.

Here's the thing however, we have to truly want to be free. If you remember above I had mentioned how when I was dealing with porn, I always knew that if I got caught, I could just ask for forgiveness and Mitzi would forgive me and God would as well and so in all actuality, I might have been sorry for getting caught, but I wasn't sorry enough to repent – to truly turn away from the sin and this is why I remained bound up in it.

We must make this distinction, because we can pray all day long, until we are blue in the face. We can cry and beg God to forgive us, but not until we are truly ready to turn away are we going to truly find victory, and then after this we must be willing to fight – to stand against the temptations that come our way.

The best way we can do this is by meditating on the Word of God – by truly allowing His Word to permeate our very beings –by falling in love with Him and the Word. Then and only then, will we begin to see victories in our life.

Our Pastor has taught us before that it is good to

learn from failures, but even better to learn from someone else's failures, and better yet he says is learning from someone else's victories! I'm not sure if he went this far, but I wanted to take it a bit further and say that even better than that would be to learn from your own victories – and this of course comes after you actually begin to have victories.

Sin is bad. It separates us from God. But, sin has been dealt with already! Jesus Christ was beaten, bruised, battered, spit upon, cursed, ridiculed, whipped, crucified – he became sin – so that we would no longer have to live under its grip!!! Sin is not the problem. Pornography is not the problem. Drugs are not the problem.

Jesus has paid the price! By believing in Him, repenting of our sin, turning to God and away from the devil, by confessing openly and boldly that Jesus Christ is our Lord and our Savior, we come out from under the bondage to sin, to sickness, even death cannot phase us because it now simply means we are absent from the body, but present with the Lord! (although I would encourage you for your sake, and also those whom God has orchestrated for you to have an impact upon and to bless and that of your loved ones, not to do things that would take you away too early).

Therefore, this is why when all we do is focus on sin and how bad it is, how bad we are or how bad everyone else is, we can never seem to get free. Why? <u>Because we are magnifying the problem instead of the solution!</u>

I want you to know something right now. God loves you. There is nothing you have done or will do that will ever, ever, ever separate you from His love for you – God is love. However, just because God is love and that He loves you unconditionally, it doesn't mean you have received it and I would encourage you to receive it!

You have read some of the struggles I have had since becoming a Christian and I'm sure some of you have wanted to reach through the book somehow and give me a nice slap (in love, of course), because you have been given the opportunity to see the big picture in just a few moments of time. You have seen in one chapter how God did some big miracle in my life and then in the very next chapter or even the end of that same one, here I am off doing something I shouldn't and paying for it.

Life isn't a book however, and we aren't so fortunate to always be able to see the big picture all at once. Sometimes, we as humans can be so forgetful and dare I say it, dumb. But praise be to God who is faithful and <u>He has the ability to see the end from the beginning</u> and what He sees is you blessed! He sees you whole! He sees you through the eyes of love! He is Love!

God is not above looking down and wagging a judgmental finger at us. <u>Instead He is waiting on us to come up to Him through what Jesus has done for us and begin to see as He does!</u> So, the problem isn't sin, just as it wasn't with the first man Adam. Adam chose sin, sin didn't choose Adam. Adam already had victory over sin; he gave away his victory when he decided to turn away from God.

Now, we have victory in Jesus and forgiveness of sins. It is our choice once again what to do with this. Will you allow sin to continue to rule you or will you allow God's power to reign in you?!

I encourage you to stop focusing on sin and start focusing on Jesus, on the Word of the Living God – only then will you ever truly be free from sin and whatever it is that has you weighed down.

For me, it was pornography, and I know there are a lot of Christians who are dealing with this right now – perhaps many who are reading this book and I want you to know that God is not mad at you. He loves you with an everlasting love and He wants to be intimate with you in a way that pornography can never bring about.

Sexual sin is so bad because it is a flagrant misuse and perversion of something that God created to be holy and good. Satan did not invent sex, he simply perverted it. The world did not invent sex, it has simply perverted it. The thief comes not but for to steal, and to kill, and to destroy, but Jesus came so that you might have life and that life more abundantly!! (John 10:10)

You can experience true freedom today, right now, but you have to truly want it. You must turn away from lust, from the lies of the enemy and delve into Truth – into God's Word. Ask for forgiveness, truly mean it from your heart and then get into the Bible, glean every scripture you can on being free form sin – on being intimate with God, allow the Word to seep into your very being. <u>Every single time,</u> a temptation comes your way; use the Word to fight it away. Give no place to the devil.

Read about David and the problems he had after lusting after another man's wife. Read the Proverbs and it talks about a man being brought so low after having given his life to lust – like a piece of bread or an ox to the slaughter.

Find purpose beyond your pain. Start doing small acts of kindness for others. You will be amazed at how easily sin melts away in your life when you stop focusing on it so much. Like Pastor Jim is always saying, "When you live a life of giving, when you focus on others instead of yourself, you will live more holy on accident, than you ever could on purpose."

It's so true! I don't want you to read this book and come away thinking that God did everything for me. Yes, He did everything for me that I couldn't do. He forgave me of sin. He died for me. He loved me when no one else did. He gave me a new heart. He made me a new creation. He has done and continues to do exceedingly and abundantly above all I could ask or think according to the power that works in me. (Ephesians 3:20)

Yet, notice that I am the one asking, I am the one thinking, I am the one that the power is working through. If you look all the way back to the first paragraph in part 2, I said that God has given each one of us unique gifts, talents, and abilities…you see God does His part. He always will. We must do ours.

Sin is not the problem. Jesus paid the price for it. You have already been forgiven. You have already been healed. You have already been delivered. You have already been given the power, the ability to love. What are you going to do with it all?

I encourage you to start receiving it. To start making one good choice after the next and over time, not overnight, you will begin to see God move so mightily in your life. Where once sin had such a grip on you and was all that you could think about, now you will be thinking about God, His word, others so much and that is what will be at the forefront of your mind.

Finally, I want to end with this and it's yet another profound and awesome thing I have learned at Joy – yet it ties in with everything we have already been talking about - if you want to be successful, if you want to begin to walk in freedom, if you want to be free from porn, from any addiction, from sin, if you want to have money, if you want a job, if you want a good marriage, if you want children, if you want a car, if you need a friend, if you want a hug, if you want to be holy, whatever it is that you want or desire so badly – if you want these things, stop searching after them!

Simply stop, take a deep breath…and pray in faith "Father, thank you for providing all these things for me already. I thank you Father that your word declares that you know what I have need of before I even ask and so Father, in Jesus' name – in the authority of Jesus Christ

– based on what He has done in me and for me, not what I have or haven't done, In Jesus' name, Father teach me to be a giver. Teach me to seek first your Kingdom and your Righteousness and I know that according to your Word, all these things will be added to me. In Jesus' name, Amen. (So be it!)

Now if you prayed that prayer and truly meant it, get ready! ☺ Get ready for God to begin to move in your life in a mighty way. Now please understand that He will more than likely start small – remember He desires a relationship with you and a relationship is a two-way street. He needs to see if you are truly serious. He may start putting your co-worker on your heart, your neighbor, your mom or dad, your siblings, your friend, your spouse, your Pastor, whomever it is and whatever it is He asks – whether it's simply to offer a smile, a hug, a small gift, an act of kindness, I encourage you to listen and obey and watch God move through you to start blessing others.

Take every single one of these things as small victories and start learning to go from victory to victory to victory instead of sin to forgiveness, sin to forgiveness.

God is so good! Thank you again for reading this book! I hope it has been an encouragement to you of God's unfailing love, His restorative power, of His love towards you, I pray that you will learn to go from simply enduring life, to loving life and that you will learn as I have to begin to <u>live joyfully ever after!</u>

By: Joshua Scott Zeitz

The Best Is Yet To Come.

"Bye, Bye, Bye, To The Old Me"

"Therefore, if any man be in Christ, he is a new creature, the old things are passed away, behold all things are become new." ~*2 Corinthians 5:17 KJV*

My Life's an open book
So hear my story
Took the time to write it out
So don't ignore me
Didn't do it for the fame
But for His glory
Shared my thoughts and my struggles
It was gory.
Now I'm soaring.
Life without Jesus
It was boring
Sin had me snoring
Same thing every night
Pass the porridge
Addicted to apples,
But needed oranges
Bananas off the foliage
Forget the trees,
YO! I smoked the forest
Opposite of whole,
I was porous
Wait! Did I just rhyme with oranges?
That was gorgeous!
Time to brag upon my God
He's enormous!

His love, it restores us
His Grace, it implores us
His Spirit exhorts us
Hid away in His fortress
Rapping slow like a tortoise
Killing beats like the orcas
Karate Choppin'
Like Norris
Off the Chain
Yo! I'm Cordless.
You don't like it?
Abort us
Keep the Bible before us
Get yours out of storage
Stop with the Taurus
My God, He's so for us
I got more just don't force us
Stomp you out like T-Saurus
Pass the thesaurus
I'm scoreless
Bye, Bye, Bye

Bye, bye, bye to the old me.
No more MeTube or half-Him.
No more used-to or has-been.
I don't need peace, I have Him.
I don't smoke trees, I half them.
I'm choppin'em up in the lyrics,
Been freed from the lust, no more limits,
I'm bad man.
In case you don't know?! Yo, that's rad man.

No more mask, got my bat man.
You don't know?!That's the Bible!
Just call me the trash man,
Tossin' sin like I'm Batman.
Wonderfully, fearfully made, I'm in His hands.
I'm on His plan.
This is His jam.
Call me a hater, dogmatic, don't faze me, I'm His friend.
I'm in His fam.
Lust and lies be damned!!
You got slammed!!
By my man Jesus Christ on the cross, He's the Lamb!
God's masterful plan of redemption, it stands!
You got glitz, you got glam, and that's grand, but it's spam.
Get your face out the cam.
You know who I am.
I'm Skippin' the chorus,
So, Stop with the shams.
Bye, Bye, Bye

You're laughin' at me, but I'm laughin' at you.
Cross bout your neck, but you ain't got a clue.
Climbing Ladders, Chasing Dollars,
Girls on your neck, but you treat 'em like garbage.
Your insides are rottenness.
I'm the gravedigger plottin' this.
The incredible hulk, yo, I'm stompin' this.
Jesus Christ on the track and I'm droppin' this.
Like a fish outta water, you're floppin' this.
You got shoes, you got clothes – yo, that's marvelous!
Where's the happiness?

Better yet, where's the Joy? Now that's fabulous!
Getting phat with this.
That's P-H-A-T, I'm Count Rapulous.
Try to bring life and you're mad at this?
Take a stab at this?
Like you Romulus?
Et tu, Brute? That's so ominous!
BFF with the Pharmacist?
Get your high, then be gone with this?
PC or not, I'm the bomb at this!
Call Me Malone, I'm the Mailman!
Christ in my life, no more jail man!
No more fail man!
Riding high on my God like a sail-man!
Swallow beats like a whale man!
You want free? It's on sale man.
Chasin' shadows, like Pan Man.
Got you under like quicksand.
So bland! Sick'nan!
Quick Man! Give Him your Hand!
You Drown'an!
Where the money at?
Bye, Bye, Bye

Look!
I don't rap cash.
I don't rap chains.
I don't rap trash.
I don't rap gangs.
I don't rap fast.
But I wrap lames.
I rap Christ.

Yo, I rap change.
I'm PB, you jelly boy!
Get your eyes off that telly boy!
I'm 'bout to will this rap nilly.
Used to Jack Jill, like a hillbilly,
So silly
Case you don't know, that's robbin' folks.
Then I got saved
it ain't a hoax.
I rap peace.
You rap jokes.
I rap Christ.
You rap toast.
Talkin' bout bread like it's the boast.
Talkin' bout fame like insta-host.
I talk about God and the Holy Ghost.
Swingin' thru the air like Spiderman.
Doing the things only Jesus can.
Here's the plan:
RIP!! to the Cold Me,
Bye, Bye, Bye to Old Me!

By: Joshua Scott Zeitz

*Joshua today...living in God's joy!
With his wife, Mitzi,
and his children;
Moriah, Isaiah, and Josiah.*

Write it out! *What is your redemption story?*

_____
_____
_____
_____
_____
_____
_____
_____
_____
_____
_____
_____
_____
_____
_____
_____
_____
_____
_____
_____
_____
_____
_____
_____
_____
_____
_____
_____
_____
_____
_____

"For I know the thoughts that I think toward you, says Yahweh [The Lord], thoughts of peace, and not of evil, to give you hope and a future." ~Jeremiah 29:11 (WEB)

"This is the day which the Lord hath made; we will rejoice and be glad in it." ~Psalm 118:24 (KJV)

"Trust in the Lord with all thine heart; and lean not unto thine own understanding.

In all thy ways acknowledge him, and he shall direct thy paths." ~Proverbs 3:5-6 (KJV)

"*Now to him who is able to do exceedingly abundantly above all that we ask or think, according to the power that works in us, to him be the glory in the assembly and in Christ Jesus to all generations forever and ever. Amen.*"
~Ephesians 3:20-21 (WEB)

"This poor man cried, and the LORD heard him, and saved him out of all his troubles." ~Psalm 34:6 (KJV)

"*Let us not be weary in doing good, for we will reap in due season, if we don't give up.*" ~*Galatians 6:9 (WEB)*

Feel free to contact Joshua Scott Zeitz by email at:

captivatedhope@gmail.com

If you are looking for a church home, check out Joy Church online:

https://joychurch.net/